"In *Taught by God*, Brandon Smith shows the Bible from the past mobilized certain in and through the text. As we discover ho. .... today, the result is not a servile deference to the past but balanced wisdom for the church's future."

—**Matthew W. Bates,** professor of theology, Quincy University

"The premodern way of reading Scripture—more accurately the universal Christian practice until around 1800—was not just a simple method, but, as Brandon Smith shows, a common set of sensibilities: paying close attention to the flow of the words, the theological-Christological focus, and with the goal of personal and communal transformation. Smith invites us to a retrieval of this common inheritance as a way forward from our present situation into the riches of the gifts of the Lord."

—**John Behr**, Regius Professor of Humanity, University of Aberdeen

"Brandon Smith's *Taught by God* is a genuine act of kindness. Marked by breadth and depth of learning, Smith ably guides readers though the halls of time, helping us sort through the strengths and weaknesses of the church's biblical reading practices. This book offers resources from Christ's church for a thick and textured reading of Scripture."

—**Mark S. Gignilliat**, professor of divinity, Beeson Divinity School

"Being 'taught by the triune God' through the Scripture is a transformative dynamic believers share in common with ancient Christians. Smith opens our eyes to the host of the church's teachers from across the centuries, whose hermeneutical work can enrich our own understanding. Smith's beautiful exposé of writers like Origen, Justin, Hugh of St. Victor, and John of Damascus makes this book a vital tool in evangelical retrieval of biblical hermeneutics that can resource each reader as well as the church at large."

—**Stefana Dan Laing**, associate professor of divinity, Beeson Divinity School

"What do figures such as Irenaeus, Chrysostom, Augustine, and Aquinas have to do with Martin Luther, John Calvin, and William Tyndale? When it comes to scriptural interpretation, Smith overthrows the myth of Reformers who turned their backs upon the church's traditional biblical exegesis, and he offers concrete examples of the interpretation of specific biblical texts."

—**Matthew Levering**, James N. Jr. and Mary D. Perry Chair of Theology, Mundelein Seminary

"Brandon Smith offers a compelling case for the retrieval of ancient Christian hermeneutics for the benefit of the modern church. The volume is a masterclass in learning from the early church for the renewal of modern Christian practice."

—**Steven A. McKinion**, professor of theology and patristic studies, Southeastern Baptist Theological Seminary

"It is such a delight to see the movement to retrieve a theological and ecclesial reading of the Bible come into maturity. This work invites us to appreciate and practice reading Holy Scripture with wise, ancient sensibilities that show our long-standing communion with the saints."

—**Jonathan T. Pennington**, professor of New Testament interpretation, The Southern Baptist Theological Seminary

"*Taught by God* offers a helpful introduction to some of the key interpretive sensibilities of early Christian interpreters. Smith not only describes early interpreters read Scripture, but also demonstrates how we can recover these sensibilities today. This is a great place to start!"

—**Stephen Presley**, Senior Fellow, Center for Religion, Culture, and Democracy

"Why should we care about premodern interpretation? After all, we don't hold to their medicine or science anymore. The answer, says Brandon Smith, is that they were taught by God how to read the word of God, and we modern Christians have much to learn from our premodern forbears, especially when it involves to our cultural and interpretive blind spots. The church would foster healthier reading habits if Christians today recovered the three sensibilities that Smith identifies as hallmarks of premodern biblical interpretation."

—**Kevin J. Vanhoozer**, research professor of systematic theology, Trinity Evangelical Divinity School

"I hope Smith's apology for retrieval anchors us. May we read pre-modern sources and model Smith's exegetical virtues of retrieval as we retrieve the exegetical traditions for the church."

—**Shawn J. Wilhite**, associate professor of New Testament, California Baptist University

BRANDON D. SMITH

Taught by God

Ancient Hermeneutics *for the* Modern Church

ACADEMIC
BRENTWOOD, TENNESSEE

To Knox, my one and only son
May you be taught by God.

CONTENTS

ACKNOWLEDGMENTS

I would not have written this book without Madison Trammel's encouragement. He and the rest of the B&H Academic crew are top notch, and it was a joy to work with them on this project. I am also deeply thankful to Mitchell Chase and Shawn Wilhite for their feedback on early drafts of the manuscript, and to Trent Rogers and J. R. Gilhooly for their feedback on my Greek and Latin translations. I owe a further debt of gratitude to Cedarville University for their support during the writing of this book, and to my church history and patristic exegesis students whose brilliant and insightful questions made this book better.

Last but certainly not least, I am constantly amazed at the triune God's grace in allowing me to live, move, and have my being. His grace is most evident to me through my wife, Christa, and our four wonderful children. God uses their unconditional love and ceaseless joy to keep me grounded and my priorities in line.

ABBREVIATIONS

1-2 Apol.   Justin Martyr, *Apologia I and II* (*First Apology and Second Apology*)

Ad. Eluc. Pent. Hugh of Saint Victor, *Adnotationes Elucidatoriae in Pentateuchon* (*Explanatory Notes on the Pentateuch*)

Ad Leand.   Gregory the Great, *Ad Leandrum* (*Letter to Leander*)

AH   Irenaeus of Lyons, *Adversus Haereses* (*Against Heresies*)

Comm. Jo.   Origen of Alexandria, *Commentarii in Joannim* (*Commentary on John*)

Comm. Pss.   Thomas Aquinas, *Commentarii in soliloquia sive hymnos Davidicos* (*Commentary on the Psalms*)

Con. Ar.   Athanasius of Alexandria, *Contra Arianos* (*Against the Arians*)

Con. Cels.   Origen of Alexandria, *Contra Celsum* (*Against Celsus*)

Conf.	Augustine of Hippo, *Confessionum Libri Tredecim* (*Confessions*)
CR	John Calvin, *Corpus Reformatorum: Johannis Calvini Opera quae supersunt omnia* (*Body of Reformers: The Works of John Calvin*)
De Doc.	Augustine of Hippo, *De Doctrina Christiana* (On Christian Doctrine)
De Fide	John of Damascus, *De Fide Orthodoxa* (*The Orthodox Faith*)
De Pot. Dei	Thomas Aquinas, *De Potentia Dei* (*On the Power of God*)
De Util. Cred.	Augustine of Hippo, *De Utilitate Credendi* (*On the Profit of Believing*)
Dial.	Justin Martyr, *Dialogus cum Tryphone* (*Dialogue with Trypho*)
Didasc.	Hugh of Saint Victor, *Didascalicon de Studio Legendi* (*Didascalicon on the Study of Reading*)
Ep.	Gregory of Nazianzus, *Epistulas* (*Epistles*)
Ep. ad Greg.	Origen of Alexandria, *Epistula ad Gregorium* (*Letter to Gregory*)
Epid.	Irenaeus of Lyons, *Epideixis tou apostolikou kērygmatos* (*On the Apostolic Preaching*)
Exp. Ps.	Augustine of Hippo, *Enarrationes in Psalmos* (*Expositions on the Psalms*)
Haer.	John of Damascus, *Liber de Haeresibus* (*On Heresies*)
Hic Est Lib.	Thomas Aquinas, *Hic Est Liber* (*Here Is the Book*)
Hom. Gal.	John Chrysostom, *Homiliae in Galatas* (*Homilies on Galatians*)

Hom. Gen.	Origen of Alexandria, *Homilies on Genesis;* John Chrysostom, *Homilies on Genesis* (*Homiliae in Genesim*)
Hom. Lev.	Origen of Alexandria, *Homiliae in Leviticum* (*Homilies on Leviticus*)
LW	Martin Luther, *Luther's Works.* Edited by Jaroslav Pelikan (vols. 1–30), Helmut T. Lehman (vols. 31–55), and Christopher B. Brown (vols. 56–75). St. Louis: Concordia; Philadelphia: Fortress, 1955.
Or.	Gregory of Nazianzus, *Orationes* (*Orations*)
PL	J. P. Migne, *Patrologiae Cursus Completus . . . Series Latina*
Princ.	Origen of Alexandria, *De Principiis* (*On First Principles*)
Praescr.	Tertullian of Carthage, *De Praescriptione Hereticorum* (*Prescription Against Heretics*)
Retr.	Augustine of Hippo, *Retractationes* (*Retractions*)
Script.	Hugh of Saint Victor, *De Scripturis et Scriptoribus Sacris* (*On Sacred Scripture and Its Authors*)
Sent. Div.	Hugh of Saint Victor, *Sententiae de Divinitate* (*Sentences on Divinity*)
Serm. Dom. Mont.	Augustine of Hippo, *De Sermone Domini in Monte* (*On the Sermon on the Mount*)
ST	Thomas Aquinas, *Summa Theologiae* (*Summary of Theology*)
WA	Martin Luther, *D. Martin Luthers Werke: Kritische Gesammtausgabe; Schriften* [Weimarer Ausgabe]. Weimar: Hermann Böhlaus Nachfolger, 1883.

	(*Martin Luther's Works: Critical Complete Edition: Writings*)
WA DB	Martin Luther, D. *Martin Luthers Werke: Kritische Gesammtausgabe: Deutsche Bibel.* Weimar: Hermann Böhlaus Nachfolger, 1906–61. (*Martin Luther's Works: Critical Complete Edition: German Bible*)

INTRODUCTION:
BEING TAUGHT BY GOD

"No one can come to me unless the Father who
sent me draws him, and I will raise him up on the
last day. It is written in the Prophets: And they will
all be taught by God. Everyone who has listened to
and learned from the Father comes to me—not that
anyone has seen the Father except the one who is
from God. He has seen the Father. Truly I tell you,
anyone who believes has eternal life." (John 6:44–47)

Christian history is a story of being "taught by God."
As we reflect on the importance of understanding
Scripture, Jesus's words in John 6 are instructive for us—they give
us a set of sensibilities for reading Scripture. First, he shows us that
the biblical text is the revelation of God and God teaches it to us by
the Son and Spirit (e.g., Luke 24:44–45; 1 Cor 2; 2 Tim 3:16–17;
2 Pet 1:21), and its claims are therefore the foundation for knowing
and obeying him. Second, Jesus tells us in John 6 and elsewhere that
the way to understand Scripture is to learn from God—namely, the

revelation of the Father through the Son and the Spirit's illumination of the truth by allowing us to "remember," "hear," and "listen" to all he has said in Scripture (Luke 24:44; John 14:26; Rev 2:7). Third, when one hears and listens to the Son and Spirit, one has "seen the Father," been "taught by [the triune] God," and has the ability to live as a disciple now and hope for the future resurrection and eternal life. In this way, any good reading or proclamation of Scripture should seek to address the three sensibilities above. Taking the summary of John 6 above as the example, "As it is written in the Prophets" signifies that (1) we should take the words, phrases, and context seriously because these are God's words to his people, and (2) we should be sensitive to theological-Christological points being made about the triune God's unified self-revelation. Further, obeying the Father and Son with an eye toward eternal life signifies that (3) we should seek to live as disciples who follow Jesus and thus are taught by God. Not only do these three sensibilities apply to this particular passage, but this particular passage can serve as a paradigmatic command from the mouth of Jesus to see all divine instruction with these assumptions in mind.

God's people—from Adam to Israel to the church—are people who are taught by God. It is his words, his wisdom, and his power that shape our understanding of the world and ourselves. When we read Scripture—the primary means by which God speaks to us—we are entering the divine classroom for sanctifying instruction. The Father speaks to us by his eternal Word, Jesus Christ the Son, and we hear their words through the illumination of the Holy Spirit. As modern Christians, we can learn from our ancient forbears because they, too, were taught by God.

In the following chapters, I will survey the premodern period of church history in order to (1) describe the underlying interpretive sensibilities shared by Christians throughout the majority of church history and, by highlighting them, (2) recommend ways modern Christians can learn from this great cloud of historical witnesses. I will first explain the premodern approach to biblical interpretation and work out a few of their presuppositions, followed by a primer on why modern Christians should care about a premodern approach in the first place.

What Is the Premodern Approach to Interpretation?

Throughout Christian history, there have been myriad theological and ecclesial debates. At various times, the church has argued at length about issues like the biblical canon, the divinity of the Son and Holy Spirit, the sacraments, the relationship between sin and grace, the role or authority of bishops, the relationship between church and state, and so forth. Sometimes these debates were settled by majority, others were settled by schisms. But if you read the sources and follow the arguments—whether in an individual's writings or in broader creedal decisions—you will find that the interpretation of Scripture was always at the center. David Dockery has usefully summarized premodern interpreters, saying, "Even though the articulation of their faith was influenced by their context, culture, tradition, and presuppositions, all shared a common belief in the Bible as the primary source and authority for the Christian faith."[1]

---

[1] David S. Dockery, *Biblical Interpretation Then and Now* (Grand Rapids: Baker, 1992), 15. Dockery, along with others like Timothy George and Stephen Holmes, was in many ways ahead of his time among

Throughout this book, I will describe ancient hermeneutics as "premodern," which is a shorthand way to talk about Christianity before the Enlightenment, beginning around the eighteenth century. Using the term *premodern* is not required in order to benefit from the following argument in this study, but it nonetheless helps situate the period of church history that I argue we should more consciously rediscover in our day. In truth, what is argued in this book spans all of Christian history, though the modern post-Enlightenment period was a noticeable blip on the Christian tradition's radar, when "critical" studies became more prevalent in Christian interpretive practices.[2]

There have been many expedient options for describing trends in premodern interpretation. One might argue that the premodern approach is largely concerned with "allegory" or "theological" readings that are detached from the "literal" sense of Scripture. Some might discuss a division between the "schools" of Antioch and Alexandria. Others might discuss the so-called "Quadriga" or fourfold sense of Scripture. Instead of or alongside these descriptions, one might assert that the Reformation was a modern shift toward

---

contemporary Baptists and opened the door for the current resurgence in theological retrieval among Baptists and broader evangelicalism.

[2] The major blip on the radar of Christian history is what we might call the "modern" or post-Enlightenment approach to interpretation, which at worst views the Bible as "just another book." Versions of this approach seek to interpret the Bible apart from, or at least without primary attention to, a divine ontology. Edgar Krentz openly concedes that the historical-critical method is a product of the Enlightenment in *The Historical-Critical Method* (Philadelphia: Fortress, 1975), 55. This is not to be confused with the historical-grammatical method, which places more emphasis on Scripture's divine ontology.

fundamentally re-ordering (or perhaps even saving the church from) patristic-medieval interpretive methods.

However, none of these options are quite right. They too easily give the impression of large-scale divisions, rather than in-house nuances between Christian figures and eras. The truth is that Christian groups can share common assumptions or confessions while also experiencing varying levels of theological and practical diversity. Indeed, with any era, figure, denomination, and movement in Christian history, it is important to recognize the difference between unity and uniformity, similarity and homogeneity. So, on the one hand, we do not have to atomize the early church such that every major thinker or era is viewed as entirely distinct and separate from the others; on the other hand, we must be careful not to flatten out church history such that every major thinker or era is viewed as essentially identical.

For example, I am in some ways a child of two theological streams. In my late teens and early twenties, I was discipled by a Wesleyan pastor and served as a youth pastor in a Wesleyan church. I read Arminius and Wesley voraciously. I saw distinctions in their theologies at times, and I realized quickly that even the broader Arminian-Wesleyan tradition is not a monolithic group, neither in theology nor practice. I noticed, for example, clear differences between the American expression of the United Methodist Church (UMC) and the small conservative Wesleyan group that I was a part of.

In my early-to-mid-twenties, I became enamored with the "Young, Restless, and Reformed" movement and developed a deep love and affinity for "Reformed" streams of Baptist life, which led me to the Southern Baptist Convention (SBC) for a large part of

my early pastoral ministry and theological development.[3] I learned
quickly, once again, that neither Reformed traditions nor Baptist
traditions were monolithic. Even within the SBC, I found rival
factions over, for example, how "Reformed" a Baptist could be—
and this is to say nothing about disagreements between and within
more classically Reformed traditions such as Presbyterianism and
Anglicanism.

Most of us who have been around the church long enough
can attest to this unity within diversity. If someone were to ask me,
"Do you Baptists believe [x]?", I might say, "Which Baptists?" But
I would also recognize that Baptists have certain core beliefs and
affirmations that make them Baptists. Baptists may disagree about
whether paedobaptism really is baptism, but all Baptists would generally agree that credobaptism is the correct or preferred mode of
baptism. Baptists may disagree about a single-elder vs. plural-elder
model, but both groups would generally agree on the importance
of local church autonomy. Baptists may disagree about how to vote
politically, but all would generally agree on the need for a separation of church and state. When it comes to Baptists, generally
speaking, you know it when you see it. There's a Baptist sensibility
that undergirds its various expressions throughout the world and
throughout the centuries.

Further, we must recognize up front that a premodern approach
is not merely a question of how to read Scripture as a literary document; rather, a premodern approach is more closely related to a
habitus, a way of living and viewing the world. This worldview,

---

[3] I might say back to the SBC, as I was baptized and began to follow
Jesus as a teen in an SBC church, but I did not understand the theology
well enough to have any real tie to it.

if I can use the term generally, grounded reading and interpreting Scripture in a set of theological assumptions about God and the world. Premodern exegetes were generally more concerned with virtue formation than academic debates about methodology. This led to a variety of individual and communal ways of reading and interpreting Scripture, even among contemporaries. And this is precisely why it is difficult and even unwise to make blanket statements about methodology in premodern interpretation.

In this book, I will approach premodern interpretation with these cautions in mind. When working through these sensibilities, we need to be aware of the underlying assumptions that premodern exegetes brought to the text about God and the world. So, while the premodern Christian tradition certainly experienced diversity, development, and debate in methodological precision and nuance, we can nonetheless identify a premodern Christian tradition that worked from a similar set of assumptions about how to read the Bible in light of theological presuppositions. So we will not overlay a specific methodology of a premodern approach; rather, we will recognize that a premodern approach arose from a robust Christian worldview centered around God and communing with God in the world. Rather than making the case that the early church—or even eras of the church—employed a uniform, homogeneous, strict methodology for its first 1800 years of existence, I will argue that these assumptions led to certain "sensibilities" that undergirded premodern interpretation. Put another way, I will avoid a narrow set of "senses" and instead survey a broader set of "sensibilities."[4] The three sensibilities are as follows: (1) letter and history; (2) theological and Christological unity; and (3) personal

---

[4] With apologies to Jane Austen.

and ecclesial communion with God. We see in these three sensibilities that premodern exegetes employed interpretive strategies from a broader way of viewing God and the world. As the book unfolds, we will survey these sensibilities at length in conversation with premodern exegetes.

Of course, not every premodern conclusion should be considered equally correct or beneficial. Premodern exegetes unsurprisingly come to sometimes radically different conclusions about the meaning(s) of the text. However, these sensibilities nonetheless characterize default assumptions when approaching interpretation.

What to Expect

Let me say up front: I do not pretend to offer a hermeneutical silver bullet here. Not every text is easily understood with this set of sensibilities, nor do they automatically fix every interpretive issue that arises. Nonetheless, I believe these sensibilities still offer promise as a part of our preparation for reading and teaching Scripture deeply and faithfully. After all, personal Bible reading, family devotionals, small group studies, sermons, and academic commentaries all engage in interpretation as they seek to understand the meaning of the text and its importance for doctrine and life.

The hope for this book is to help modern Christians better understand our spiritual forebears so that we might glean from them. Premodern Christians were sometimes as diverse as Christians today, and yet we all bear the mark of Christ and we live our lives heavenward as people of the Book. This Book is God's revelation so that we might know him and might live in light of who he is. If so, then these three sensibilities should feel as natural to us as breathing. We might even say that they represent the rhythm of our spiritual breathing as we read God's Word. In the end, as our forebears before us sought to proclaim, when we read the Spirit-inspired Scriptures as Spirit-filled people, we can be taught by God as we read.

In the following chapters, I will engage with several figures throughout church history under the heading of each sensibility. In introducing these sensibilities, I want to let our premodern forebears speak and then encourage modern Christians to respond. My goal is to introduce and summarize the premodern biblical interpretation fairly so that we can learn from those who came before us, without flattening out history or underemphasizing the distinctions between figures and eras. In an attempt to maintain this balance, the structure of the book will be as follows.

Chapter 1 is a (very brief) history of interpretation to orient the reader to the most obvious shifts throughout the premodern period as a way to prime the pump for the sensibilities covered in the book. Chapters 2–4 will consider each sensibility. These chapters highlight a select group of theologians throughout the premodern period, showing how the sensibility took shape in interpretations of Scripture. Each of these chapters will close with an exhortation for why this sensibility is important for modern Christian interpretation. Chapter 5 will explore a handful of reasons why looking back at the premodern approach can help modern Christians move forward. Chapters 6–9 will conclude our study with four examples (not prescriptions) of how one might utilize these sensibilities in exegeting a biblical text.

At times throughout church history, there was an overlap in the sensibilities because, in part, it is difficult to separate them from one another. While the fourfold sense might be the most well-known exegetical strategy, those who employed it would not have imagined that the sensibilities underneath the method could be separated from one another. And this is partly the point of this present book. Labels such as "allegory" or "history" do not always mean the same things to different people, either those who are contemporaries with one another or those who are centuries apart. Some used a twofold method; others threefold; others fourfold; and still others did not explicitly explain general methodology. But these sensibilities remain the same across the Christian tradition precisely because they are Christian questions—questions prompted by Christ and the Scriptures. Let us consider these sensibilities as one way to be faithful to his Word.

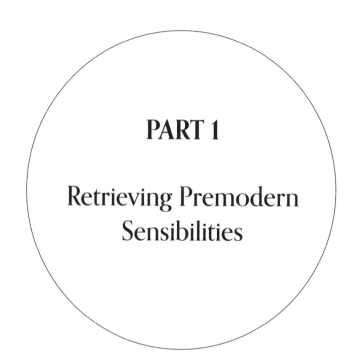

PART 1

Retrieving Premodern Sensibilities

1

A (Very Brief) History of Interpretation

As I mentioned at the outset, Christian history is a story of biblical interpretation. If we want to understand why the early church came to its theological and ecclesial conclusions—many of which we take for granted as obvious truths—we need to understand how the early church read their Bibles. This will be a difficult task, because the Christian tradition is not entirely monolithic or linear. Indeed, perhaps all the books in the world could not contain the story of biblical interpretation in church history, but there are notable shifts in interpretive methods and emphases represented by larger shifts in the church and the broader culture.

The goal of this chapter is to briefly introduce these major shifts as a basic orientation for the reader, as well as a way to set the stage for the three sensibilities we will discuss in the bulk of this book. I have divided the history of interpretation in the premodern period into three parts: the patristic era, the medieval era, and the Reformation era. The following brief history will help orient us to the more nuanced conversations in the following chapters.[1]

History of Interpretation

Patristic Era (AD 100–600)

The earliest Christians sought to follow the pattern of interpretation laid out by the apostles and their writings. A group of writers and documents now called the Apostolic Fathers includes letters and theological treatises from the late first century into the second century. Most of these writings quote a wide array of New Testament (NT) books; others were likely written around the same time as some of the NT books. For example, *1 Clement* was likely written right near the end of the first century, possibly around the time NT books like John's Gospel or Revelation were being written. Traditionally attributed to Clement of Rome, this letter quotes or alludes to around fifteen NT books. Other early Christian leaders, like Polycarp of Smyrna, were said to have learned from the apostles

---

[1] These three divisions of history are admittedly disputable but need not detain us long. Some end the "Patristic Era" as early as AD 450 (around the convening of the Council of Chalcedon) and as late as AD 800 (after the closing of all seven ecumenical councils). I think AD 600 serves as a good transition marker toward a more Medieval theological and philosophical culture. Others would break up the "Medieval Era" into "early" and "late" periods, or use the term "Middle Ages." Still others might also extend the "Reformation Era" by another century. I have chosen to keep the divisions somewhat broad for our introductory purposes here.

themselves.[2] Most of these works resemble NT epistles to churches or individuals, with words of encouragement, theological teaching, and related issues, particularly in relation to the church's persecution at the hands of the Roman Empire.

Second-century Christians saw persecution from the Roman Empire increase. A group called the Apologists rose up during this time to plead for Christian freedom and distinction among the Greeks and the Jews. For our purposes, Justin Martyr is perhaps the most notable among them. Three of his works address interpretive issues: two of them—*1–2 Apologies*—deal with Scripture and Greco-Roman philosophy, while the other one—*Dialogue with Trypho*—interacts with a Jewish man regarding Christianity and the Old Testament (OT). In Justin's works, we get a glimpse into the budding rhetorical and literary debates over interpretations of Scripture and relevance for Christian life in Rome. When dialoguing with the Greeks, he shows that Scripture offers a "philosophy" that is greater and more coherent than the prevailing Greco-Roman platonic thought, drawing on the unity of Scripture.[3] When debating Trypho, he does not lay out a specific interpretive method, but his basic argument is that the words of the OT refer to Christ and thus are Christian Scripture.[4]

Another second-century theologian, Irenaeus of Lyons, battled against Gnostics who claimed that their gospels were equal to or

---

[2] Polycarp sat under John's teaching, according to Irenaeus (*AH* 3.3) and Tertullian (*Praescr.* 32.2).

[3] *1 Apol.* 22. He notes, for example, that certain Greek figures like Mercury and Perseus have stories that resemble Christ's life, but Christ is obviously their superior. This is part of a larger case for Christianity as a legitimate philosophy worthy of respect and freedom to practice.

[4] *Dial.* 29–33.

superior to the four Gospels the church had accepted. Whenever there was a contradiction, their false gospels won the day. Irenaeus argued, however, that Scripture is a unified whole, like a mosaic that displays the image of a beautiful king. And because the Gnostics introduced contradictions and heresies with their own gospels, they made the mosaic into an image of an ugly dog or fox.[5] Third century theologian Origen of Alexandria argued similarly for the unity of Scripture as God's revelation, while introducing a more intentional exegetical method of "letter" and "spirit"—a way of reading Scripture that does justice to the literary and historical claims of Scripture (letter), while digging deeper to see the theological mysteries that drew Scripture together in Christ (spirit). We will return to Irenaeus and Origen in subsequent chapters.

Justin, Irenaeus, Origen, and others modeled what would be called "the rule of faith"—a shared assumption throughout much of the Christian tradition that Scripture is inspired by the triune God and thus is a non-contradictory, unified witness to him.[6] The rule of faith clarifies an important point: the patristic writers did not appear to make a true distinction between exegesis and theology. In certain circles of modern scholarship, there is a strong bifurcation between interpretation and theological construction. For some, theology is an unnecessary add-on to exegesis, either because the Bible is "just another historical document" or because "all we need are the words of the text, not man-made doctrines." Patristic

---

[5] *AH* 1.8.1.

[6] For a helpful introduction to the development of interpretive techniques as a way to challenge false teaching, see Lewis Ayres, "Irenaeus vs. the Valentinians: Toward a Rethinking of Patristic Exegetical Origins," *Journal for Early Christian Studies* 23/2 (2015): 153–87.

writers roundly rejected any such distinctions or, for that matter, even acknowledged their existence. For them, Scripture is divinely inspired and thus totally true, authoritative, and unified.[7]

It was once popular to describe two developing streams of exegetical methods or interpretive emphases in the third to fourth centuries as rooted in the "schools" of Antioch (more "literal") and Alexandria (more "spiritual" or "allegorical"). However, the differences between them have been greatly exaggerated, and calling them "schools" indicates that more systemization was present in either place than really existed.[8] It is fairer to say that the differences between exegetes writing and teaching in Antioch and Alexandria consisted in nuances in the general tenor of their burgeoning academic rhetorical and literary environments—something we could call a "reading culture" or, per Peter Martens, an "exegetical culture."[9]

---

[7] Space does not allow an extended discussion on the development of the biblical canon in the early church. For a good introduction, see John D. Meade and Peter J. Gurry, *Scribes and Scripture: The Amazing Story of How We Got the Bible* (Wheaton, IL: Crossway, 2022).

[8] This exaggeration comes in part from the assumption that Origen's exegetical foes were Antiochene disciples. However, those "friends of the letter" that he wrote against appear to have been wholly opposed to the spiritual sense, but this was not true of the Antiochenes; see Henri de Lubac, *Scripture in the Tradition*, trans. Luke O'Neill (New York: Crossroads, 2000), 47–48. We will discuss this further in later chapters.

[9] Peter W. Martens describes the scene in Antioch as an "exegetical culture," which it seems could also be applied to Alexandria; see Adrian's *Introduction to the Divine Scriptures: An Antiochene Handbook for Scriptural Interpretation*, Oxford Early Christian Texts (Oxford: Oxford University, 2017), 15–16. Indeed, as Martens points out, if there is a "school" in Antioch, it would be tied to a few major figures: Diodore of Tarsus, John Chrysostom, and Theodore of Mopsuestia, but the term "school" nonetheless has too much baggage to overcome. See also, Frances M. Young, *Biblical Exegesis and the Formation of Christian Culture* (Cambridge:

An Antiochene like John Chrysostom placed more emphasis on the historical narrative of Scripture (particularly Israel's story) and the moral implications. An Alexandrian like Origen generally placed more emphasis on "allegorical" or spiritual readings of Scripture, which some critics both in his own day and after his death considered too arbitrary or loose. And yet, in the case of figures in both Antioch and Alexandria, one should recognize that exegetes in both places were concerned with the letter and spirit, even though some emphases might differ. The difference was related more to rhetorical and literary practices in their respective contexts than deep-seated theological or exegetical distinctions. Thus, "reading cultures" or "exegetical cultures" allows for more nuance than an organized bifurcation that "schools" might indicate, and then the reader must take the next step of letting any figures in any era speak for themselves.

Consider the relationship between John Chrysostom and Origen. In their Genesis homilies, John Chrysostom sees the suffering and resurrection of Christ in the Noah narrative; Origen talks at length about the historical truthfulness of God's command to Noah and the ark's measurements as the foundation for the spiritual sense.[10] If one bought into the idea that these Antiochene and Alexandrian "schools" are vastly different, one might assume these

---

Cambridge University, 1997), 186–212. Though scholars like Martens have built upon her work, the discipline of early Christian studies owes Young a debt of gratitude for being a gateway to seeing that the Antiochene and Alexandrian schools were more similar than previously argued.

[10] I owe John C. Cavadini for this comparison in "From Letter to Spirit: The Multiple Senses of Scripture," in *The Oxford Handbook of Early Christian Interpretation*, ed. Paul M. Blowers and Peter W. Martens (Oxford: Oxford University, 2019), 141–42.

interpretive moves by Chrysostom and Origen would be switched; however, for early Christians across the known world, Scripture was considered divinely inspired and thus the letter and spirit were assumed to be inextricably linked. This basic assumption carried on through the fourth-century debates over the deity of Christ and the Holy Spirit, with the myopic, "literal" exegesis of figures like Arius challenged by a more balanced approach to the relationship between letter and spirit among the pro-Nicenes. Indeed, the famous theological debates of the fourth to fifth centuries were ultimately centered on biblical interpretation.

The later patristic period stands under the shadow of one towering figure: Augustine of Hippo, a North African bishop living in the late fourth to early fifth century. Augustine's exegetical method is notoriously difficult to generalize, in part because we have access to over 500 extant sermons, as well as several books and treatises that span a career marked by theological and pastoral seasoning. The closest center of his method is probably his most well-known contribution to premodern interpretation: what is now called "semiotics." Semiotics deals with how signs and symbols function in interpretation. In short, Augustine sought to describe a distinction between "signs" (*signa*) and "things" (*res*).[11] There are things—such as wood or stone—that are not signs in and of themselves; they can stand alone as objects with no signification. However, some things are also signs when used that way by biblical authors—such as the

---

[11] *De Doc.* 1.2.2. Augustine's fourfold sense of the OT is also important to consider, wherein he says that the OT's fourfold sense is history, etiology (signification in names or titles), analogy, and allegory (signifying Christ and/or the church); see *De Util. Cred.* 3. Interestingly, however, Augustine never appears to return to an explicit fourfold approach as his career progresses, and it makes no appearance in *De Doc.*

ram that Abraham sacrificed instead of his son, which was a thing
that signified deeper realities about salvation in God's economy.
Further, a sign is a thing that is used to signify something else. And
since all words are ultimately signs that describe actual things in
the world, biblical interpretation requires an attentiveness to what
the words signify, with these biblical signs pointing to the ultimate
thing: the triune God.

These signs in Scripture ultimately point toward a spiritual
reality. For example, the Jews missed Christ's significance because
they mistook signs for mere things and thus allowed the "letter"
to blind them to the signs or deeper spiritual realities unveiled in
the incarnation. Here he quotes a common passage in Christian
interpretive tradition, 2 Cor 3:6: "The letter kills, but the Spirit
gives life."[12] They did not recognize, for instance, that the law's sacrificial system ultimately pointed to Christ's sacrifice on the cross.
We might call this "allegory" for Augustine, given that he views
allegory as the Christological and/or ecclesiological referent in the
OT;[13] however, Michael Cameron has helpfully and more specifically called this sensibility "the Christological substructure of
Augustine's figurative exegesis," noting that toward the end of
the fourth century, he eventually saw the OT as "less distinguish-
able from the New" and beginning "to function pastorally and

[12] *De Doc.* 3.5.9. For a helpful discussion on Paul's hermeneutics and
their reception, see Matthew W. Bates, *The Hermeneutics of the Apostolic
Proclamation: The Center of Paul's Method of Scriptural Interpretation*
(Waco, TX: Baylor University, 2012).

[13] See *De Util. Cred.* 3.

polemically [as] the first book of the New Testament."[14] In other words, Augustine's approach to Scripture as a unified witness to God in Christ permeated through all of his work. Augustine's impact cannot be overstated, as he clearly influenced later great figures such as the Victorines, Thomas Aquinas, Martin Luther, and John Calvin. We will return to Augustine in later chapters.

A final figure worth noting is Gregory the Great, a Benedictine monk and the bishop of Rome from AD 590–604. In many respects, Gregory acts as the bridge figure between the patristic and medieval eras. He was an inheritor of the theological and exegetical tradition of the past, while at the same time reforming and advancing the church's liturgy and missionary zeal. For our purposes, his threefold method of interpretation is of most importance. In a letter to Leander, he notes that his interpretive method consists of the literal-historical sense (the words and history of Scripture), the allegorical sense (theological-Christological), and the moral sense (contemplation, communion, and transformation).[15] While this multi-sense approach was not entirely new in the history of interpretation—one thinks of John of Cassian's fourfold method, for example[16]—his commentary on Scripture resonates with the more systematized process that became prevalent in the medieval period.

---

[14] Michael Cameron, "The Christological Substructure of Augustine's Figurative Exegesis," in *Augustine and the Bible*, ed. and trans. Pamela Bright (Notre Dame, IN: University of Notre Dame, 1986), 74–75.

[15] *Ad Leand.* 1.

[16] See, for example, his fourfold description of Jerusalem in *Conferences* 8. He applies a fourfold shape to other issues such as prayer and the effects of sin.

Medieval Era (AD 600–1500)

The *Quadriga* is well-known as a crucial interpretive scheme of the medieval era, especially among the scholastics.[17] The *Quadriga's* four senses are: literal (historical), allegorical (theological or spiritual), tropological (moral), and anagogical (eschatological).[18] As we saw above, these four elements of the *Quadriga* were present throughout the first centuries of the church. Keith Stanglin rightly notes:

> Medieval exegetes, like their patristic forerunners, assumed many of the same basic principles that affect biblical interpretation: the divine inspiration, unity, and transformative purpose of Scripture; the necessity of a spiritual and virtuous interpreter; and the church's rule of faith as the key to proper interpretation. In this and similar ways, medieval exegesis is simply a continuation of patristic exegesis.[19]

The medieval fourfold sense was still undergirded by the preceding Christian tradition. Indeed, one should always remember that the

---

[17] This does not mean that every figure after AD 600 used the *Quadriga*, nor does it mean everyone who used the *Quadriga* used it the same way. Nonetheless, many of the most influential figures self-consciously utilized this fourfold method.

[18] Perhaps the definitive work on medieval exegesis is Henri de Lubac's four-volume *Exégèse médiévale*. Of particular note is the first volume on the four senses, which can be found in English: Henri de Lubac, *Medieval Exegesis, Vol. 1: the Four Senses of Scripture*, trans. Mark Sebanc (Grand Rapids: Eerdmans, 1998).

[19] Keith D. Stanglin, *The Letter and Spirit of Biblical Interpretation: From the Early Church to Modern Practice* (Grand Rapids: Baker Academic, 2018), 78.

Christian tradition, even with its variety, shares in common these default assumptions about the nature of Scripture and, in turn, the way an interpreter should approach the text. Medieval interpreters also often utilized the patristic creeds and writings as sources of authority and interpretive guardrails.

Nonetheless, it is fair to say that medieval biblical interpretation became more systematized both in theory and practice in comparison to the preceding centuries, in large part due to the flourishing academic environment across the medieval world. And while biblical commentaries had been produced throughout the Christian tradition, the medieval period introduced a wave of innovative commentaries and glosses (notations in the margins or between the line of a particular text). These works took on various forms, from the more intentionally "literal" commentaries and glosses of Theodore of Tarsus's seventh-century Canterbury school, to the more allegorical longform commentaries of Bede and the eighth-to-ninth-century Carolingian Renaissance.[20] Like the Antiochene-Alexandrian distinction, medieval interpretive "school" distinctions can be exaggerated; however, the various intramural academic debates over interpretive method certainly introduced more complexity and diversity of emphases than previous centuries.

The Victorine school of interpretation was another notable and influential school during the later medieval era. Hugh of Saint Victor's career as an academic—both in the classroom and writing—was set against particular strands of medieval interpretation that

---

[20] Theodore and his colleague, Hadrian of Canterbury, had an affinity for the "Antiochene" commentaries/homilies of figures like John Chrysostom and Theodore of Mopsuestia.

became too unhinged from the letter in their pursuit of allegory. Influenced by Augustine's signification theory, Hugh was a proponent of multiple senses of Scripture, though he defended the literal sense as the foundation for any allegorical or spiritual sense.[21] This zeal for the letter was generally due to Hugh's concern for the primacy of Scripture's authority, and perhaps more specifically his concern for rigorous and careful exegetical methodology. His concern for methodology also extended to an attentiveness to the great theologians of the past, particularly figures such as Origen, Jerome, Augustine, Isidore of Seville, and others.[22] This methodological rigor led to intramural debates over particular text even within the Victorine school, such that not every Victorine commentary is monolithic; nonetheless, a careful, step-by-step application of the *Quadriga* largely defines the school.[23] We will return to Hugh in later chapters.

The greatest theologian-philosopher of the medieval period, Thomas Aquinas, wrote several biblical commentaries and also compiled commentaries of patristic authors. He, too, sought to recover a concern for the letter in the midst of medieval allegorical excess. Following Augustine, Thomas was not concerned with reconstructing the human author's mind or context. Indeed, both

---

[21] William M. Marsh, "Scripture and Tradition," in *Historical Theology for the Church*, ed. Jason G. Duesing and Nathan A. Finn (Nashville: B&H Academic, 2021), 166–67.

[22] *Script.* 6.

[23] For example, Richard and Andrew of Saint Victor followed Hugh's lead on interpretive theory and practice, though they at times disagreed on what the literal sense did and did not entail; see *Interpretation of Scripture, Theory: A Selection of Works of Hugh, Andrew, Richard and Godfrey of St Victor and of Robert Melun*, ed. Franklin T. Harkins and Frans van Liere (Hyde Park, NY: New City, 2013), 41–46.

Augustine and Thomas assert consistently that this information is ultimately unknowable—all that can be expected is for the interpreter to render a meaning that is faithful to Christian doctrine and fitting with the text's flow of logic and reasoning. So, though one cannot reconstruct the historical situation and thought process of the author without a time machine, one can understand the author's "intent" insofar as the author signals important literary threads that allow the text to be divided and organized toward its intended end goal.[24] Thus, to remain faithful to the letter is to ensure that the spiritual senses or meanings do not abandon orthodoxy or a "plain" understanding of the letter. Reconfiguring Augustine's "things" and "signs," Thomas notes that "words" and "things" are both signs under the inspiration of the divine author. As such, the words and things described by the words are the literal or historical sense of the *Quadriga*. This literal sense is the sense from which the spiritual sense must be drawn in order to avoid confusion or contradiction. For Thomas, the spiritual sense—the things signified by the words and things—has a three-fold division of (1) allegorical (when the Old signifies the New), (2) moral (what we ought to do), and (3) anagogical (what relates to eternal glory).[25]

Nicholas of Lyra (AD 1270–1349) is a notable figure toward the end of the medieval era, especially due to his influence on the remainder of the medieval era and into the Reformation era as an

---

[24] For a helpful overview of these similarities between Augustine and Thomas, see John F. Boyle, "Authorial Intention and the *Divisio textus*," in *Reading John with St. Thomas Aquinas: Theological Exegesis and Speculative Theology*, ed. Michael Dauphinais and Matthew Levering (Washington, DC: The Catholic University of America, 2005), 3–8.

[25] *ST* I, q. 1, a. 9.

influence on Martin Luther's work.[26] His influence is primarily
seen in the ongoing relevance of his *Postilla Litteralis*—a set of notes
on the literal sense of Scripture—which was often appended to a
prominent collection of glosses often called the *Glossa Ordinaria*.[27]
Nicholas is still firmly medieval in his approach to the fourfold
sense, which he famously outlines in the form of a poem or rhyme
(in Latin):

> The letter teaches events,
> allegory, what you should believe;
> tropology, what you should do;
> anagogy, where you should aim.[28]

Nonetheless, Nicholas introduced the idea of a "double-literal"
sense in relationship to Christ and the OT, using the example of
Solomon and Christ. In his well-known example from 1 Chronicles
17, Nicholas comments on God's promise to Solomon: "I will be
his father, and he will be my son." He comments that Solomon as

---

[26] For example, Luther refers to Nicholas 127 times in his commentary on Genesis. Luther commends Nicholas as the best among medieval interpreters given his focus on the literal-historical sense. Luther also moves away from Nicholas by critiquing him for allowing the Church Fathers to, at times, sway him too far into allegory at the expense of the literal; see WA 42:71. For a thorough account of Nicholas's influence on Luther, see Thomas M. Kalita, "The Influence of Nicholas of Lyra on Martin Luther's Commentary on Genesis" (PhD diss., The Catholic University of America, 1985).

[27] Frans van Liere, *An Introduction to the Medieval Bible* (Cambridge: Cambridge University, 2014), 166–67.

[28] "*Littera gesta docet, quid credas allegoria, quid agas tropologia, quo tendas anagogia.*" This appears in different forms, but notably in his prologue to *Postilla Litteralis*. This also resembles John Cassian's fourfold description noted above.

the "son" is the literal sense of that passage. However, the author of Hebrews also quotes this passage, applying it to Christ (Heb 1:5), so this statement is also literally about Christ. This double-literal sense is to be distinguished from an approach that would treat the sonship of Solomon as the literal sense, but the Christ-fulfillment as the "spiritual" sense.[29] For Nicholas, the literal sense was concerned with literary elements, historical context, and authorial intent, but the meaning was not isolated to the historical context and authorial intent because God is still the providential author of the biblical canon. Nicholas's work was still popular during the rise of the Reformation era, and his double-literal sense paved the way for certain interpretive moves in the Reformation—most notably as Luther would later similarly identify Christ as the literal sense of all of Scripture.

Reformation Era (AD 1500-1600)

The Reformation era marked another shift in premodern interpretation—a shift that was perhaps more seismic than in any era before, given the context of the Protestant Reformation. Like the medieval era, the Reformation era not only ushered in a noticeable development in biblical interpretation, but also spawned a new culture in the world at-large, aided by separation from the Roman magisterium, the expansion of preaching, and advancement in printing technology. However, it is an exaggeration to say that the Reformation marked an abandonment of premodern sensibilities, or sparked the dawn of the "modern" age of hermeneutics. Most

---

[29] Nicholas also published a less-influential tropological interpretation of texts called *Postilla Mystica seu Moralis*.

notably, the Reformers moved away from the *Quadriga* as a systematized methodology, but retained many of the same emphases of eras past.

David Steinmetz offers a helpful and thorough "ten theses" of Reformation hermeneutics:

- The meaning of a biblical text is not exhausted by the original intention of the author.
- The most primitive layer of biblical tradition is not necessarily the most authoritative.
- The importance of the Old Testament for the church is predicated upon the continuity of the people of God in history, a continuity which persists in spite of discontinuity between Israel and the church.
- The Old Testament is the hermeneutical key that unlocks the meaning of the New Testament and apart from which it will be misunderstood.
- The church and not human experience as such is the middle term between the Christian interpreter and the biblical text.
- The gospel and not the law is the central message of the biblical text.
- One cannot lose the tension between the gospel and the law without losing both gospel and law.
- The church that is restricted in its preaching to the original intention of the author is a church that must reject the Old Testament as an exclusively Jewish book.
- The church that is restricted in its preaching to the most primitive layer of biblical tradition as the most

authoritative is a church that can no longer preach from
the New Testament.

• Knowledge of the exegetical tradition of the church is an
indispensable aid for the interpretation of Scripture.[30]

Steinmetz's list highlights the continuity between the Reformation
era and the preceding Christian tradition. For example, the first
thesis argues that the Reformers still recognized that God's providence in history governs the biblical storyline and thus the two
Testaments exist in an inseparable relationship. As we have seen
above, this unified biblical storyline was part-and-parcel with
Christian readings of Scripture from the beginning. Therefore, they
did not abandon the spiritual sense—reading as a Christian still
demanded that Christ be the center and fulfillment of Scripture.

Summarily, one could say that the focus on the letter and history continued to undergird or subsume the spiritual sense(s) in the
Reformation era, particularly in relation to the unity of the biblical canon and the Christological key to understanding its unity.
Moreover, the Reformers were not called the Destroyers; they did
not seek to destroy the previous 1,500 years of Christian tradition,
but rather sought to reform the late medieval church and re-center
the church on the authority of Scripture and its patristic-early
medieval roots.[31] The Reformers were thus undoubtedly "premod-

---

[30] David C. Steinmetz, "Theology and Exegesis: Ten Theses," in
*Histoire de l'exégèse au XVIe siècle: textes du colloque international tenu à
Genève en 1976* (Switzerland: Droz, 1978), 382.

[31] Luther, for example, was certainly, at times, critical of patristic theology and the excesses of medieval allegory, but he nonetheless openly
appreciated and relied upon the Christian tradition. Beyond his positive

ern" (or, in Steinmetz's term, "pre-critical") in their approach to biblical interpretation, seeing themselves as inheritors of the rule of faith. Luther, for example, was not ardently opposed to allegorical readings as some might assume, but rather opposed to certain types of allegory that were clearly beyond the bounds of Scripture and the rule of faith.[32] Ultimately, Luther collapsed the fourfold sense into a single literal sense, because he saw the literal sense as containing not only literal and historical elements, but also Christ himself, as Scripture's Lord and teacher.[33]

Reformation biblical interpretation also frequently centered on the relationship between the two "Words"—"Law" and "Gospel." If one compares Luther and John Calvin—the leading lights and lasting figureheads of the Reformation—the similarities and dissimilarities between them are obvious. In terms of similarity, they both agree that Scripture consists of these two Words and that they cannot be separated from one another. However, the notable

---

use of Nicholas that we noted above, he also positively—though not uncritically—interacted with other premodern figures like Augustine and Jerome in other works; see the helpful chart of references in his Galatians commentary provided by David C. Fink, "Martin Luther's Reading of Galatians," in *Reformation Readings of Paul: Explorations in History and Exegesis*, ed. Michael Allen and Jonathan A. Linebaugh (Downers Grove: IVP Academic, 2015), 30.

[32] For example, Luther says famously in an excursus on Genesis, "When we condemn allegories we are speaking of those that are fabricated by one's own intellect and ingenuity, without the authority of Scripture. Other allegories which are made to agree with the analogy of faith not only enrich doctrine but also console consciences" (LW 2:164).

[33] For a detailed study on the relationship between the rule of faith, premodern interpretation, and exegetical practice in Luther, see Todd R. Hains, *Martin Luther and the Rule of Faith: Reading God's Word for God's People* (Downers Grove: IVP Academic, 2022).

distinction is one of emphasis. For Luther, the Law and Gospel operate in a synchronic relationship, such that there is a command and promise in both Testaments, so that *Law* and *Gospel* are not merely shorthand for "OT" and "NT" since both Testaments contain both Words; Calvin, on the other hand, saw the two Words in a diachronic relationship, describing a type of redemptive-historical movement from promise to fulfillment.[34]

The Reformation emphasis on *sola scriptura*, the literal sense, and "Christ-centered" hermeneutics became the dominant staple of Reformation era commentaries, theological works, and pulpits. Nonetheless, the Reformation era carried on the sensibilities of the Christian tradition. We will return to Luther, Calvin, and others in later chapters.

Toward a Rediscovery of Premodern Interpretation

Throughout the premodern church's diverse and disparate methodologies, interpretive strategies, exegetical conclusions, and contextual arguments was a set of shared sensibilities that characterized the types of questions Christians asked when reading their Bibles. This brief history of interpretation has oriented the reader to some general trends in early Christian interpretation. This orientation should allow the following chapters to be more digestible.

---

[34] I owe these categories of synchronic and diachronic to Michael S. Horton, "Theologies of Scripture in the Reformation and Counter-Reformation: An Introduction," in *Christian Theologies of Scripture: A Comparative Introduction*, ed. Justin S. Holcomb (New York: New York University, 2006), 85.

The point of this book is not to prescribe a specific methodology, nor to idolize premodern exegetes as infallible interpreters of Scripture. Instead, I hope the brief survey above and the examples in the following chapters will add fuel to the fire of renewed interest in the Christian tradition, and foster a recognition of modern Christians' place among this great cloud of interpretive witnesses. The subsequent chapters will highlight a selection of premodern exegetes on each of these three sensibilities as a way to introduce readers to premodern exegetical thought and practice, as well as highlighting the importance of these sensibilities for modern exegetes. In the end, my hope is that modern Christians see these sensibilities as questions we are already prone to consider in exegesis. As we allow our forebears to help us hone our interpretive methods and conclusions, I pray that we may be more and more faithful to the Scriptures. Now, we turn to chapters that lay out the three sensibilities of premodern interpretation in more detail.

2

Which Way Do the Words Go?: Letter and History

Christians are a people of the Book.

The words written by various authors over many, many years are the bedrock of our faith. These biblical words are the words we read, sing, teach, and memorize. They shape Christian grammar. Thus, letter and history have served as the foundation of biblical interpretation throughout the Christian tradition. The question "Which way do the words go?" underlies all biblical interpretation because these words are the words we interpret. They are the words passed down to us.

In light of this, it is no surprise that a concern for "the way the words go" was always a fundamental sensibility in the premodern approach to biblical interpretation.[1] This concern is often called the "literal sense" or "letter" or "history," and seeks to understand the literary and historical features present in the actual words of the biblical text. When we read words, we are naturally following the way the words go. But the concern rises above mere words, because we are also ascertaining the "meaning" of those words.

Much of modern biblical interpretation consumes itself with this very concern.[2] We ask questions such as, "What did the original author mean?", "How would the original audience have understood this text?", and "Is this describing an historical event/person?" We often seek to answer these questions through word studies, literary analysis, historical recreation, archaeological verification, and other "scientific" means.[3] This concern among modern interpreters is not an entirely bad impulse—as we were taught in grade school, the "five W's" help us ask the most basic questions in the text. And, indeed, premodern exegetes often asked similar questions. The difference between the premodern exegetes and modern exegetes is a matter of emphasis and contextual concern. For example, in a post-Enlightenment world, it seems incumbent on Christians today to verify the historicity or historical veracity of the Bible's claims, especially when the competing world of ideas feels so dominated by the scientific revolution. Defenses for Scripture's historical or factual

---

[1] This phrase is drawn from Thomas Aquinas's "*salva circumstantia litterae*" in, for example, *De Pot. Dei* 4.1c.

[2] For a watershed article on the shift from "pre-critical" to modern exegesis, see David C. Steinmetz, "The Superiority of Pre-Critical Exegesis," *Theology Today* 37/1 (1980): 27–38.

[3] By "scientific," I simply mean that we employ controlled methodologies to come to conclusions based on empirical observation and/or evidence.

claims made appearances at times in premodern writings, but the emphasis and urgency for apologetic purposes pales in comparison to commentaries and debates today. Moreover, when many of the premodern exegetes talk about "history," they are talking about the events described in Scripture rather than a more modern instinct to try to reconstruct past events.

Likewise, in terms of literary analysis, premodern exegetes were generally not as concerned with Paul's writing style or a psycho-analysis of the original hearers' potential perceptions. Instead, pre-moderns often were attentive to word studies and linguistic details to the extent that it helped them make sense of the textual coher-ence and general argument of the biblical text. When interpreting a passage, premodern exegetes were interested in what the text says as a way to understand what the text means (one would be hard pressed to find a strict distinction here). Origen of Alexandria, for instance, pored over various translations of the Bible and created his *Hexapla*—a six-columned work containing six translations of the Hebrew Bible—as a theological project as much as a literary project. In the end, he sought to best understand the correct words of the Hebrew Bible so that Christians could teach the Bible cor-rectly and defend the Christian faith. Origen was not alone in this endeavor; from Irenaeus to Jerome of Stridon to Martin Luther, it was commonplace to develop canon lists that outlined the author-ity of certain texts and biblical translations that ensured the church's access to the biblical text.

So, these questions that moderns often ask were not absent in the premodern period; some discussed the literary details of the text or the historical veracity of biblical claims. The difference is primar-ily a distinction in emphasis and significance. Stanglin is correct in asserting, "Early readers and hearers of Scripture were not less

attentive to details than their modern counterparts; rather, they
sought and found a different significance in the details."[4] When
premodern authors—especially those in the patristic era—discussed
the "way the words go," they were willing to assert that God had
ordered the words in such a way that they could be interpreted
in multiple ways and/or with various levels of meaning or significance. As such, grammatical skills were necessary to understand
God's revelation because Scripture's depth required intellectual
(and spiritual) rigor. Lewis Ayres, using the terms "grammatical"
and "figural" to discuss the letter/spirit relationship, notes:

> These categories [of grammatical and figural] are not
> mutually exclusive: grammatical techniques are also used
> within figural practices. Grammatical techniques are, how-
> ever, the fundamental reading tools, essential for the good
> reading of scripture.[5]

This is a different emphasis than some modern forms of the "literal
sense" that look for a single, unalterable meaning that can only be
found by recreating the human author's intentions and context. I
would not argue for abandoning some advancements in modern
biblical studies regarding text criticism and historical contextual
data, but rather assert that these cannot be the final questions. In
any event, whether a premodern interpreter called this sensibility
"letter" or "history" or something else, the questions and assumptions are generally the same—using grammatical, literary, rhetorical, and historical tools to bring the "plain" meaning of texts to bear.

---

[4] Stanglin, *The Letter and Spirit of Biblical Interpretation*, 49.
[5] Lewis Ayres, "Patristic and Medieval Theologies of Scripture: An
Introduction," in *Christian Theologies of Scripture*, 15.

In Origen of Alexandria, John Chrysostom, Hugh of Saint Victor, and Martin Luther, we will see this sensibility play itself out in distinct but similar ways.

Origen of Alexandria

Origen of Alexandria was a third-century theologian and scholar, primarily teaching and writing in Alexandria and Caesarea. Origen's bent toward "allegorical" interpretation has become legendary, if nothing else because some reports of his wild allegory have been exaggerated to the level of fable. No doubt, Origen's spiritual readings are core to his interpretive project; however, the exaggeration occurs when one assumes that he cares nothing about the "letter" of the text at all, but rather chases allegorical rabbit trails far away from the text.[6]

For Origen, the "letter" typically means the literary or historical data in the text, whereas the "spirit" typically encompasses a range of sensibilities regarding Christological fulfillment and prefiguring and/or moral instruction. The letter serves as the foundation for the spiritual meaning, because the spiritual meaning is empty without first understanding the words themselves. Moreover, Origen

---

[6] Origen's allegory is often more tropological (moral) than Christological, because one who understands the spiritual sense (under which allegory resides) proves to be more spiritually mature in their faith. His well-known "threefold interpretation" of body, soul, and spirit—which is sometimes falsely assumed to be his hermeneutic in toto—is primarily theological and tropological, describing how one advances from basic edification (body/letter) to deep spiritual insights (soul/spirit) through the Holy Spirit, prayer, and deep study of the text; see, for example, *Princ.* 4.2.5–7; *Ep. ad Greg.* 4.

uses the tripartite analogy of body (letter) and soul/spirit (spirit) to describe Scripture, showing that Scripture *just* is letter and spirit.

Oftentimes, Origen's discussion about the letter and spirit is directly related to the relationship between, generally, the OT and NT and, more specifically, the law and Christ. In his *Homilies on Leviticus*, he introduces the relationship between the letter and spirit by comparing it to the incarnation:

> What was seen in [Christ's flesh] was one thing; what was understood was something else. For the sight of his flesh was open for all to see, but the knowledge of his divinity was given to the few, even the elect . . . so here with the veil of the letter, so that indeed the letter is seen as flesh but the spiritual sense is hiding within is perceived as divinity.[7]

Perhaps the central organizing principle for Origen's interpretive method is this incarnational model: to deny the divine inspiration of the OT and NT is to deny the whole Christ, human and divine.[8] This unity of revelation and salvation is central to understanding the method and motive of Origen's exegesis.[9] The Jews who want to continue following the law "literally" and ridicule the spiritual sense will miss the point of the law altogether. However, those who

---

[7] *Hom. Lev.* 1.1. English translations are from Origen, *Homilies on Leviticus 1-16*, trans. Gary Wayne Barkley (Washington, DC: The Catholic University of America, 1990). I am indebted to De Lubac for noting *Hom. Lev.* as a clear example of this framing in *History and Spirit: The Understanding of Scripture According to Origen*, trans. Anne Englund Nash (San Francisco: Ignatius, 2007), 104–5.

[8] See also *Con. Cels.* 6.77 and *Comm. Jo.* 1.

[9] See Rowan Williams, "Origen: Between Orthodoxy and Heresy," in *Origeniana Septima*, ed. W. A. Beinert and U. Kühneweg (Leuven: Leuven University, 1999), 3–14.

turn to Christ will have "the veil of the letter" removed by the Holy Spirit "that we may be able to behold the spiritual and wonderful knowledge of his Law . . ."[10] Origen quotes both 2 Cor 3:16–17 and Ps 118:18 here to show that God's people understand the true meaning of the Law only after the "veil" is removed from their hearts. This insistence on the letter pointing toward or undergirding the spiritual is consistent for Origen across his works. As Henri de Lubac points out, Origen asserts in a later homily that he wants to defend the letter as vigorously as the spirit because, "One must believe, first of all, in general, that things happened as they are recounted."[11]

For Origen, the letter/law already contains Christ and his words concretely, but in a veiled mystery that was not totally unveiled until the incarnation:

> And by the words of Christ we mean not only those which he spoke when he became human and dwelt in the flesh; for even before this, Christ, the Word of God, was in Moses and the prophets. For without the Word of God how could they have been able to prophesy of Christ?[12]

In another place, Origen argues similarly that Moses and the prophets were the initial "growth" or "fruits" of Scripture. However, the Gospels are the firstfruits of Scripture, which are the best pick of the harvest offered once the fruit becomes ripe: "For after all the

---

[10] *Hom. Lev.* 1.4.

[11] De Lubac, *History and Spirit*, 105; see *Hom. Lev.* 14.3: "But we who are Israelites in both parts defend both the letter and spirit in the Holy Scriptures . . . one must neither curse according to the letter nor blaspheme according to the spiritual understanding."

[12] *Princ.* Pr.1.

fruits of the prophets until the time of Jesus Christ, the perfect word sprouted forth."[13] The letter is fundamental to interpretation precisely because it sets the stage for (and is reinterpreted by) the divine Son stepping into human history. Anyone—Jew and Gentile—can see Christ in his flesh walking and talking; it is quite another thing to confess him as the divine Son and Lord. In the same way, one can read the law and ascertain basic moral principles or historical data; it is quite another to see and walk in Christ and his teachings contained there.

Additionally, the Holy Spirit's inspiration and illumination of Scripture is also crucial for his method. In *On First Principles*, Origen offers an extensive explanation of his doctrine of inspiration and its relationship to interpreting the letter and spirit. At the core is that the Scriptures—Old and New Testament—"are divine, that is, inspired by the Spirit of God."[14] The inspiration of the Holy Spirit is key for Origen's method, because people have "given themselves over to many errors" because they deny the spiritual sense of the Scriptures.[15] Again, Origen asserts that the Holy Spirit gives the ability to understand the spiritual sense—the true or deeper meaning of the Scriptures.

---

[13] *Comm. Jo.* 1.14 . My translation of: "Μετὰ γὰρ τοὺς πάντας τῶν προψητῶν χαρποὺς τῶν μέχρι τοῦ κυρίου Ἰησοῦ ὁ τέλειος ἐβλάστησε λόγος." Greek sourced from Origène, *Commentaire sur Saint Jean, Tome I,* Sources Chrétiennes 120 (Paris: Cerf, 1966), 64. Origen goes on to clarify that the Gospels are the orienting interpretive principle because, though the OT and the NT epistles are divinely inspired, "they are surely not comparable to 'Thus says the Lord Almighty'" (οὐ μὴν παραπλήσια τῷ Τάδε λέγει χύριος παντοχράτωρ).

[14] *Princ.* 4.1.1. English translations are from Origen, *On First Principles*, 2 vols., ed. and trans. John Behr (Oxford: Oxford University, 2017).

[15] *Princ.* 4.2.1.

Moreover, Origen's view of the letter is not merely a law-Christ distinction, but it also concerns more broadly the historicity of biblical claims. Origen is at times willing to question the historical veracity of certain claims or the usefulness of the law, but he also clarifies: "We are clearly resolved that the truth of history can and ought to be preserved in the majority of cases."[16] This includes portions of the law that should reasonably be followed unless it has been abolished or made impossible; things written about Jesus that were accomplished "perceptibly"; and historical details such as Abraham's burial in the cave at Hebron, Shechem as a real city given to Joseph, Solomon's temple in Jerusalem, "and countless other things."[17] So, on the one hand, "there are many more passages which stand firm according to history than those which contain a purely spiritual sense" but, on the other hand, "with respect to the whole of the divine Scripture all of it has a spiritual meaning, but not all of it has a bodily [literal] meaning" because the literal meaning is not always reasonable or possible.[18] In short, all of Scripture has a spiritual meaning because it is divinely inspired, but the passages that are purely spiritual without a genuine literal meaning are rare.

Though he wants to generally affirm the historicity of the biblical narrative, he points out that Israel and Jerusalem not only speak of historical places and people, but also are portrayed as heavenly or spiritual ideas and places in the NT—the New Jerusalem

---

[16] *Princ.* 4.3.4. The exceptions seem to be those which cannot be explained or unbound by reason. We will see below why Origen is willing to abandon the historical claims in certain cases.

[17] *Princ.* 4.3.4.

[18] *Princ.* 4.3.4–5.

as the heavenly city for all of God's people as a prime example.[19]
Where a specific detail does not seem possible either logically or
historically, Origen surmises that God inserted "certain impossi-
bilities and incongruities" as "obstacles" in order to push the reader
down "a loftier and more sublime road."[20] In doing so, the Holy
Spirit pushes the reader to consider a deeper meaning "worthy of
God." Since the Scriptures are inspired, the words and their claims
are important, but the end goal is contemplating the deep mysteries of God. Whenever Origen denies the historicity or factual
accuracy of a text, he does not assume it is a defect on the part of
Scripture's truthfulness or authority; rather, it is a divinely inspired
means of spiritual formation that the letter alone cannot or does
not convey.[21]

Origen's *Homilies on Genesis* offer another clear example of
how he relates the letter and the spiritual. He begins his homily
on Noah and the ark with a painfully detailed recounting of the
ark's measurements. Why? Because "what is related about it literally" serves as the "foundation" so that "we can ascend from the
historical account to the mystical and allegorical understanding of
the spiritual meaning . . ."[22] This natural move from the "letter" to
the "spiritual" is common for Origen in part because he is often

---

[19] *Princ.* 4.3.8.

[20] *Princ.* 4.2.9. Origen might be thinking here of the "stumbling
block" of the cross in Rom 9:33.

[21] One might think here of his famous claim in *Princ.* 4.3.1 that the
events of Genesis 1–2 do not represent actual events but rather are a sem-
blance of history for spiritual instruction.

[22] *Hom. Gen.* 2.1. English translations are from Origen, *Homilies
on Genesis and Exodus*, trans. Ronald E. Heine (Washington, DC: The
Catholic University of America, 1982).

responding to heresies or false interpretations, whether the Jews, who deny Christ and the NT, or the Gnostics, who deny the inspiration of OT.[23] In either case, the letter acts as a controlling function, because the divine inspiration of both Testaments means that their words and claims are authoritative.

After walking through the measurements and details of the ark's construction, Origen addresses a question raised by Apelles, a disciple of the influential Gnostic teacher Marcion: "How could two of every kind of animal fit onto such a relatively small boat?" Being a Gnostic, Apelles "wishes to show that the writings of Moses contained nothing in themselves of the divine wisdom" nor "the work of the Holy Spirit." Origen responds first by defending the letter: Moses was educated by the Egyptians, and an Egyptian geometrical "computation" would actually allow for the ark to fit all of the animals. So, for Origen, a basic understanding of Moses as an historical figure helps one affirm the basic truthfulness of mundane historical details like the ark's measurements.[24] Origen does not dismiss the way the words go in order to get onto juicy allegorical details, but is rather willing to argue from the historical details on their own terms. Then, of course, Origen will "ascend to the spiritual meaning" through connecting Noah's story with Jesus's story, but even then, he does so through the clear allusions in Matthew 24

---

[23] Gnosticism took many forms both inside and outside of Christian circles, so descriptions of their beliefs vary. We do, however, have extensive interactions with Marcionites from not only Origen, but other early Christian theologians like Irenaeus and Tertullian. All of their descriptions match this general accusation that they rob the OT of his divine inspiration. Apelles's variations on Marcionite teaching can be found in, for example, Tertullian's *On the Prescription of Heretics*, 30.

[24] *Hom. Gen.* 2.2.

and Luke 17.[25] But even as he unpacks the spiritual sense, the letter is the "foundation," as he makes clear.

These examples serve to show that Origen's treatment of the letter is the foundation for his interpretive work. Origen cannot separate his view of Scripture from God's economy of salvation, and the definitive moment of God's economy of salvation is the incarnation of the Son.[26] Origen starts with the words of Scripture, seeks to understand their meaning literally and historically, and then launches from there to the spiritual sense.

We should note that Origen does not simply tell the Jews that the OT should be interpreted entirely "spiritually" (allegory, typology, or otherwise) because the incarnation has rendered the letter of the OT entirely irrelevant; instead, he argues that Christ is contained in the letter, though veiled. Similarly, he does not tell the Gnostics that the OT does not really matter, so long as one confesses Jesus as Lord; instead, he argues for the historicity of the OT's claims on their own terms before he moves to the spiritual sense. In arguing against the Jews, Origen emphasized that the letter in the OT had a reference beyond the wording or factual claims, but nonetheless contained the Spirit. In arguing against the Gnostics, Origen emphasized that the OT contained the Spirit, but could not be emptied of the letter.

Ultimately, for Origen, the incarnation is the absolute paradigmatic unveiling of God's divine mysteries contained in Scripture. The letter is the foundation, but it almost always points beyond itself because Scripture is ultimately spiritual as divine revelation. As such, one cannot stop at the historical narratives or facts; one

---

[25] *Hom. Gen.* 2.3ff.

[26] Origen often used the title "Word of God" as well.

must understand them in light of God's providence and revelation of himself. Thus, contemplation on Scripture is crucial for a mystical union with God. And as one grows in faith and dependence on the Holy Spirit, one deepens their understanding of the spiritual sense.

John Chrysostom

As I mentioned in chapter 1 and showed in Origen's writings above, the Antiochene/Alexandrian divide has been greatly exaggerated, but there was nonetheless a distinct hermeneutical inflection between two figures from these areas.[27] Of course, Antiochenes were not themselves monolithic. For example, John Chrysostom, a fourth-century bishop born in Antioch and ministering in Constantinople, could at times sound more like Origen than fellow well-known Antiochene commentator, Theodore of Mopsuestia, who more rigidly denounced allegory.[28] Nonetheless, Antiochenes

---

[27] We mentioned Frances Young's contribution to understanding the Antiochenes in the previous chapter. John Behr further elucidates the "rhetorical" approach of the Antiochenes: "In this 'rhetorical' approach, interpretation of a text begins with setting out its *hypothesis*, the subject-matter at hand; the lexical level is examined next, establishing the correct punctuation and construal of sentences; attention is then paid to questions of translation and etymology, foreign words, metaphors, and figures of speech; and finally the interpreter turns to the train of thought in the text, comparing it to other texts, which might provide further background material, from the scriptures, to set the text in its proper context"; see *The Case Against Diodore and Theodore: Texts and Their Contexts*, ed. John Behr (Oxford: Oxford University, 2011), 37.

[28] There is a healthy scholarly debate about the similarities and distinctions between Chrysostom and Theodore. Donald Fairbairn rightly notes that Antiochene figures are not homogeneous, so the distinctions

like John and Theodore were generally not opposed to spiritual or allegorical readings; rather, they often emphasized that these readings should be rooted in clear intertextual connections given by Scripture itself, to varying degrees and depending on the text.

Chrysostom actually means "golden-mouthed" in Greek, and he is known first and foremost as a skilled preacher. And like so many in the premodern tradition, Chrysostom's understanding of the relationship between the "literal" and "spiritual" was tied closely to the incarnation—the humanity and divinity of the Son served as the principal analogy for seeing Scripture as inseparably literal and spiritual. Chrysostom employed two Antiochene principles in his interpretation: (1) ἱστορία (*historia*: history), which described the "literal" or historical narrative of the text (not to be confused with mere historical facts), and (2) θεωρία (*theoria*: contemplation; to behold or witness), which sought to recognize the "spiritual" reading, which included Christological, typological, prophetic, and virtuous insights in Scripture illumined by the Spirit. Thus, *historia* is important in Chrysostom's works, but *theoria* cannot be easily positioned against Alexandrian allegory as two diametrically opposed ideas. Christians in both areas recognized the need for a Christian reading that takes seriously the reality of the incarnation and its implications for a unified biblical story.

---

between Chrysostom and Theodore should not be surprising. He argues specifically that their respective Christologies played an important role in their differing exegetical practices; see Donald Fairbairn, "Patristic Theology and Exegesis: The Cart and the Horse," *Westminster Theological Journal* 69/1 (2007): 3–11.

Consider these two statements by Chrysostom in back-to-back homilies on Genesis:

> You see, despite the use of such precision by Sacred Scripture [regarding the garden of Eden], *some people have not questioned the glib words of arrogant commentators and farfetched philosophy*, even to the extent of denying Holy Writ and saying the garden was not on earth, giving contrary views on many other passages, *taking a direction opposed to a literal understanding of the text*, and thinking that what is said on the question of things on earth has to do with things in heaven. . . . Sacred Scripture, though, whenever it wants to teach us something like this, *gives its own interpretation, and doesn't let the listener go astray.*[29]

> [Jesus] then said, "Good people will be as brilliant as the sun in the kingdom of their Father." . . . So when we hear something like that, *let us not stop short at the literal level;* instead, let us reason from the perceptible and visible realities to the superiority of spiritual realities in particular. Accordingly, if it is possible to discover the keener desire and the more heightened sweetness in this case (*these sayings being, after all, divine and spiritual, and thus capable of prompting in the soul great spiritual joy*), let us with great yearning and strong desire apply our ears to the words so

---

[29] *Hom. Gen.* 13.13. English translations are from John Chrysostom, *Homilies on Genesis 1–17*, ed. Thomas P. Halton, trans. Robert C. Hill (Washington, DC: The Catholic University of America, 1990), emphasis mine.

that we may gain from them for ourselves true wealth and welcome many seeds that will germinate into right thinking about God, and thus make our way home.[30]

In the first instance, Chrysostom derides those who claim that the garden of Eden was not an actual earthly place, even though Moses uses specific words and descriptions to highlight its materiality. The descriptions, he reasons, are plain to understand and there is no need to try to strain immaterial explanations to make it more fanciful. In the second instance, he shows that David and Jesus both use language that obviously points beyond the material realities—for example, his metaphor of the sun's brilliance is obviously not to be taken entirely "literally," as though Christians will actually be the sun and/or its brilliance. As is common across Chrysostom's works, he is doggedly committed to allowing the text to restrain the extent to which the reader seeks a fuller meaning. It also shows his shared sensibility with all premodern exegetes: because Scripture is divinely-inspired, readers should not be surprised that there are deeper realities being signified in Scripture.

To flesh out an example of Chrysostom's concern for "the way the words go," we will now turn to his homilies on Genesis 16–21 and Galatians 4. Galatians 4 was and still is a central point of discussion on the relationship between the OT and the NT, notably because Paul uses the word "allegory" (ἀλληγορούμενα) in v. 24 regarding the story of Sarah and Hagar from Genesis 16–21. Chrysostom preached homilies on both texts, and drawing these two homilies together provides an example of Chrysostom's concern for the letter and history, even as he reckons with the spiritual

---

[30] *Hom. Gen.* 14.4, emphasis mine.

reading Paul invites in his epistle. Indeed, in an earlier homily, he warns his readers that the two must not be separated: "I beseech you, let us never pass heedlessly by the contents of Sacred Scripture, but even if it is a list of names or an outline of history let us descry carefully the treasure hidden there."[31]

In his homily on Genesis 16, Chrysostom seeks to understand the literary and historical context for Abraham's relationship with both women. He starts the homily by exhorting his hearers to consider this text as a teaching on harmony in marriage: "This passage, in fact, is capable of instructing both men and women to give evidence of harmony in relating to each other and to preserve inviolate the bond of marriage . . ."[32] Chrysostom then scrupulously interrogates every word and phrase of the text to draw out the reasons for God's including Hagar in Abraham and Sarah's story, becoming convinced that Abraham's patience and gentleness with Sarah and his seeming reluctance to procreate with Hagar is an example of virtue for all. For Chrysostom, Abraham sought harmony with his wife to the point that he ultimately tried to give her a child illegitimately; the suffering evident in Sarah's indignation leads to much rejoicing at the coming of Isaac. In the end, Chrysostom says, this story highlights how God providentially uses both patience and affliction to highlight his goodness.

In his next homily, he continues the story: "Why did God delay so long [in giving Isaac to Abraham and Sarah]? Not simply that we should get to know the just man's endurance and his

---

[31] *Hom. Gen.* 24.1. English translations are from John Chrysostom, *Homilies on Genesis 18–45,* ed. Thomas P. Halton, trans. Robert C. Hill (Washington, DC: The Catholic University of America, 1990).

[32] *Hom. Gen.* 38.1–2.

great virtue, but for us to see as well the extraordinary degree of [God's] power."[33] Chrysostom draws here on "what Moses teaches under the inspiration of the Holy Spirit"[34] by summarizing and moralizing the story in its own context, highlighting the larger context of Abraham's story, Abraham's age, and the various locations in which the story takes place. These literary and historical notes highlight for Chrysostom the text's emphasis on God's providence and promise-keeping to Abraham and offer a textual roadmap for following the point.

While we may disagree with Chrysostom's interpretation of Abraham's situation, it is important at this juncture to notice that, thus far, Chrysostom preaches a homily-and-a-half on the story of Abraham, Sarah, and Hagar before he mentions Christ at all. Contrary to some stereotypes of premodern exegetes, his focus on the literal-historical aspects of the Genesis story restrains him. As he works to "apply" the text or draw out its implications, he stays fixed on God's dealings with Abraham as recorded by Moses. As we saw above, *theoria* is not a textually-detached and a poor stereotype of "allegory"; rather, it is a textually-informed contemplation on the message of the text, not merely the literal-historical details. The *historia* does, however, serve as the foundation and controlling mechanism for drawing out the *theoria*. Now, toward the end of his second homily on the story, he turns to the Christological implications of the *theoria*.

The sign of circumcision in Abraham's story serves as the occasion for Chrysostom to begin to interact with Galatians. Because God knew his people would disobey and rebel against him throughout their forthcoming history,

---

[33] *Hom. Gen.* 39.5.
[34] *Hom. Gen.* 39.4.

he gave them a perpetual reminder with this sign of circumcision, as though fastening them in a chain, and set limits and rules to prevent them overstepping the mark instead of staying within their own people and having no association with those other peoples but rather keeping the patriarch's line uncontaminated, so that in this way even the fulfillment of the promises could be achieved for their benefit.[35]

This literal, physical sign originating in Abraham is God's setting them apart only for a period in history; however, Chrysostom notes that the Jews would eventually misuse the sign of circumcision to deny Christ's person and work. He then quotes Gal 5:2–4 to make the point that, "The reason, you see, for the Lord's coming was to cancel all these things, and the reason for his fulfilling the entire Law was to replace the observance of the Law in future."[36] What is the relationship between the Old and New for Chrysostom? He expands on this in his homilies on Galatians.

We now return to the point above: Paul uses the word "allegory" in Gal 4:24 in relation to the story of Sarah and Hagar. Chrysostom is first quick to note, "Contrary to usage, he calls a type an allegory; his meaning is as follows; this history not only declares that which appears on the face of it, but announces somewhat farther, whence it is called an allegory."[37] Here Chrysostom clarifies that allegory has a particular meaning apart from what may be used elsewhere— *allegory* simply means "type," a historical referent in history with a fuller meaning that is now present in Christ and the church. Thus, Paul uses Sarah and Hagar as "types" of things to come. In this

---

[35] *Hom. Gen.* 39.14.
[36] *Hom. Gen.* 39.19.
[37] *Hom. Gal.*, on Gal 4:24.

case, Hagar is the bondwoman who gives birth to bondmen "born of the Old Covenant"; Sarah is the free woman who presents the "Jerusalem that is above [which] is the Church."[38] This is most obvious, Chrysostom reasons, in the fact that the Jews live in bondage to the "Law," whereas the "Church" comprises Gentiles who were once "barren" of God's knowledge—he also cites Isa 54:1 for this barrenness motif—but now, like Sarah, have innumerable offspring. More than that, just as Ishmael persecuted Isaac, so too the Jews persecute the church.[39]

In his third and final Genesis homily directly addressing the subject, he encourages his hearers: as those who "received circumcision through baptism," Christians should "not be worse than the ungrateful, unresponsive Jews" by ignoring God's purposes and promises.[40] Instead, they should desire "the blessing and promise that the God of all made to the patriarch" and "adhere to our own ways of virtue and when mingling with [outsiders] we attract them to religion, and through a life of good works we may become the occasion of instruction for them."[41] Instead, Christians should accept Christ as the law-keeper and ultimate Son of promise, who set them free to live joyful and grateful lives.

This survey of Chrysostom's homilies on Sarah and Hagar shows his shared sensibility with Origen on the importance of both the literal-historical aspects of the biblical story and the fuller meaning contained therein. For our purposes here, we can generally

---

[38] *Hom. Gal.*, on Gal 4:25–26. Chrysostom reasons here that Hagar's name means "Sinai" and thus she is literarily-historically tied to Israel.

[39] *Hom. Gal.*, on Gal 4:27–31.

[40] *Hom. Gen.* 40.17.

[41] *Hom. Gen.* 40.1, 17.

see that Origen was interested in uncovering both the obvious and the mysterious intertextual connections in Scripture, whereas Chrysostom appears more restrained to what the text more "plainly" gives him. In both cases, letter and history drive their spiritual readings, regardless of the tools they use to draw out the implications.

Hugh of Saint Victor

In the medieval period, the literal-historical aspect of the text was not always at the center. However, Hugh of Saint Victor and his Victorine school stand out as ardent defenders of the literal sense as the foundation for biblical interpretation. In his threefold approach, he is concerned with the literary-historical ("letter" or "history"), allegorical, and tropological ("moral") senses. While much of medieval exegesis continued the tradition that the letter was the foundation, this was not always the case in practice. Hugh's insistence on going back to the literal-historical as the foundation was highly influential in the medieval period.

In *On Sacred Scripture*, he scolds those who teach allegory but care nothing for the letter:

> I wonder how some people dare to present themselves as scholars of allegory when they do not even know the first meaning of the letter. They say, "We read Scripture, but we do not read the letter. We do not care about the letter, for we teach allegory." How can we read Scripture and not read the letter? If we take away the letter, what is Scripture?[42]

---

[42] *Script.* 5. Unless otherwise noted, English translations of Hugh's work are from *Interpretation of Scripture, Theory*.

He emphasizes the importance of the literary-historical sense in his *Didascalicon* as well. He tells his students, "I do not think you can be perfectly perspicacious with regard to allegory unless you have first been grounded in history."[43] What is the historical information one should seek from the text? Hugh says, "especially . . . the person, the deed, the time, and the place."[44] Hugh warns his students not to quickly move past these features—similar to the five W's mentioned above—in a race to find the allegorical or moral senses. Further, when he mentions "history," he also broadly includes literary features such as grammar, rhetoric, dialectic, and the basic meanings of words.

An example of Hugh's exegesis can be found in his notes on the Pentateuch. Near the beginning, he sets the stage for his exegesis by emphasizing that "Moses is an historian in this book" who also tells of prophetic events.[45] Here, Hugh particularly notes that his prophetic message covers both what happened before the creation of mankind and the future blessings promised to Jacob. This historian-prophet role is important for interpreting Moses's writings because, according to Hugh, "through this historical narrative, we are brought to the understanding of higher things."[46] The literary-historical sensibility, then, keeps the interpreter focused on the text.

---

[43] *Didasc.* 6.3.

[44] *Didasc.* 6.3.

[45] *Ad. Eluc. Pent.* 3. My translation of "Moyses in hoc libro est historio." All translations from *Ad. Eluc. Pent.* are mine, sourced from the Latin text in PL 175:29–86.

[46] *Ad. Eluc. Pent.* 3. "per istam historicam narrationem ad altiorum rerum intelligentiam provehimur."

Before he launches into exegeting practically the entire book of Genesis, he states Moses's basic intention: "[Moses's] aim in this book is to demonstrate three things: primarily, God as the Creator, the creation of matter, and its formation; and all of this for the praise of God and for man's benefit, for whom it is useful to admire and give veneration to God."[47] For Hugh, then, the primary point of Genesis is to show that God created and formed all things, that we might worship God alone. Throughout his notes on the Pentateuch, Hugh at times expands his commentary to allegory or tropology, but primarily meticulously explains the literary-historical details, at times referencing Hebrew sources for his historical claims or defining basic terms used in the passage.

However, as noted above, the scaffolding for Genesis is the theological point that God is Creator and worthy of worship. After all, Hugh sees Scripture ultimately as the sacred revelation of God for our salvation, so a mere history lesson is not enough.[48] "What Moses intended" is not the primary point in the end. Hugh's threefold method is foundationally God-centered. As he explains to his students, "You have in history the means by which to marvel at the works of God, in allegory the means by which to believe in His mysteries, and in morality the means by which to imitate His perfection."[49] These "mysteries" that allegory elucidates are primarily found in "the mystery of the Trinity because

---

[47] *Ad. Eluc. Pent.* 4. "Intentio ejus est in hoc libro, tria principaliter ostendere. In primis Deum Creatorem, et materiam creatam et formationem ejus, et totum hoc ad laudem Dei, et utilitatem hominis: cui utile est Deum admirari et venerari."

[48] *Script.* 1.

[49] *Didasc.* 6.3.

Scripture also teaches . . . that God existed as three and one before every creature."[50] In his notes on Genesis, he takes the creation account to be basically historical—both in terms of past events and in terms of God's providential ordering of things. He comments on the days as though they happened successively and describes the minute details of what is created and how it relates to other created things.

He also says that Moses makes no mention of heavenly things like angels; instead Moses describes Adam's creation from the mud "as an historian focusing on visible things."[51] When he comes to Gen 1:26—"let us make man in our image"—his threefold approach comes together. Hugh explains that being made in God's image indicates mankind's unique dignity as one who shares in a characteristic of God himself. He draws this conclusion from the grammar of the text: "By the plural verb ["let us"], the distinction of persons; by conjoining the singular "our image and likeness," the unity of essence."[52] We see in his approach, then, a focus on the letter, to the point that even his theological deductions are built from literary-historical arguments. His trinitarian explanation for Gen 1:26 is a type of allegory for Hugh because it deals with the mystery of the Trinity, but he draws the conclusion from first

---

[50] *Didasc.* 6.4.

[51] *Ad. Eluc. Pent.* 7. "sed sicut historiographus de visibilibus intendit."

[52] *Ad. Eluc. Pent.* 7. "per verbum plurale distinctionem personarum; per hoc quod subjungit singulariter ad imaginem et similitudinem nostram, unitatem essentiae." This idea of being restored to the image of the Trinity—particularly to the image of the divine wisdom, the Son—is core to his work in *Didascalicon*; see *Didasc.* 2.1.

parsing the words of text themselves.[53] Of course, one does not draw the doctrine of the Trinity from an isolated reading of Gen 1:26, but his allegorical conclusion and theological confession is proven by the text's claims. He then proceeds to discuss what it means to be made in God's image and likeness as a means of salvation and contemplation.

Hugh taught his students to pursue the truth primarily through meditating deeply on the Scriptures. Ian Christopher Levy points out, "Closely aligned with meditation is the cultivation of memory, which itself forms the heart of the exegete."[54] For Hugh, then, one may not find all three "senses" in every text; however, a strong deposit of biblical knowledge not only helps the reader have the wisdom to navigate interpretive questions, but also allows the exegete to grow in virtue. Those who skip the letter to search for allegory skip that important interpretive and meditative step, for allegory is only legitimate (biblical!) if birthed out of the letter.

Martin Luther

Martin Luther is well-known as a major instigator of the sixteenth-century Reformation and as the figurehead of Protestantism. While his contributions to Protestant theology and ecclesiology are legion, he also introduced a nuanced understanding of the literal sense to

---

[53] Hugh's theological and exegetical approach is grounded in the conviction that God is the first cause of all things and has made us in his image, which is clearly taught in Genesis 1; see *Sent. Div.*, part three, which was likely written by Hugh or his pupils.

[54] Ian Christopher Levy, *Introducing Medieval Biblical Interpretation* (Grand Rapids: Baker Academic, 2018), 139.

the premodern exegetical tradition.[55] As noted in chapter 1, Luther's framing of Scripture as two "Words"—"Law" and "Gospel"—is in many ways the orienting principle of his approach to interpreting the Bible. The easiest way to summarize this approach is to simply say: Christ is the literal sense of Scripture. The prefaces to Luther's commentaries shed significant light on Luther's interpretive inclinations. In William Marsh's extensive study on the prefaces, he explains that

> Luther's prefaces for his German translation of the Bible are indispensable source material to comprehend this Reformer's thought, and taken together, they form a holistic picture of Luther's essential theology of Scripture *and* his view of Scripture's theology. . . . [The] "prefaces" support the conclusion that Luther ultimately considers Christ as the literal sense of Scripture because of the Bible's messianic unifying thread.[56]

Marsh notes, for example, that Luther's preface to the NT (1522) describes the relationship between the OT and NT. Both are "books" in their own right, but the "Gospel" is contained in both, since the Christ preached by the apostles is the "true David" who defeated sin, death, and the devil.[57] In his preface to Romans—"a

---

[55] For a brief argument for Luther as a premodern figure, see Kenneth Hagen, "Luther, Martin (1483–1546)," in *Dictionary of Major Biblical Interpreters*, ed. Donald K. McKim (Downers Grove: IVP Academic, 2007), 692–93.

[56] William M. Marsh, *Martin Luther on Reading the Bible as Christian Scripture: The Messiah in Luther's Biblical Hermeneutic and Theology* (Eugene, OR: Pickwick, 2017), 34–35, emphasis original.

[57] Marsh, 37–38; see *LW* 35:358; WA DB 6:4.

controlling document for how one ought to read and to interpret the rest of the NT"—Luther identifies "Christ as the *textual referent* of the promise God made to Adam and Eve" in Gen 3:15, when he promised them a future serpent-crushing seed.[58] These two examples show that Luther pulls the "spiritual" sense(s) under the heading of the literal sense.

This point can be seen further by examining Luther's interpretation of Psalm 118 (1530). Luther begins the commentary by highlighting the goodness of the Lord and the historical and canonical situation in which David writes this psalm:

> Although he had the finest laws and customs, established by God through Moses, to aid him, together with the prophets who had anointed and confirmed him as king by God's command, he had learned by experience what the power and wisdom of kings and princes can do in a nation if God Himself does not lend a hand. Absalom, his own son, and later Bichri taught him who was king in the land. Likewise Daniel declares (4:17; 5:21): "The most high God rules over the kingdom of men and sets over it whom *He will*." Not whom we will or think. Daniel is simply saying that temporal government is purely and solely a gift and grace of God, which no man can establish or maintain by his own wisdom or strength.[59]

Luther sets the stage by first locating David's own words in their context. David recognized through his own life and the lives of other rulers in Scripture that he could rule Israel only through the

---

[58] Marsh, 42–43; see *LW* 35:369; WA DB 7:8, emphasis mine.
[59] *LW* 14:53–54, emphasis original.

Lord's wisdom and grace. David's praise to the Lord is, for Luther, deeply theological and borne from experience.

The psalmist turns toward the audience's response in v. 4: "Let those who fear the LORD say, 'His faithful love endures forever.'" Luther follows the way the words go by also turning his commentary toward the audience when the psalmist does. He interprets "those who fear the LORD" as "the elect children of God and all the saints on earth, the genuine Christians. For them this psalm was especially written, and of them it speaks to the very end."[60] At this juncture and for several following verses, Luther explains that Christians must praise the Lord even through the sufferings and trials of life, for this is the calling of all who follow the Christ who himself suffered. And those who follow Christ have the eternal hope of redemption and life with God.

The commentary takes a sharper Christ-centered or typological turn at v. 16, in which David says that the Lord's right hand is "exalted" and "does valiantly." Luther builds from this a threefold description: (1) "it does valiantly," meaning, it delivers us from sin and the devil, and leads us to salvation; (2) "it is exalted," meaning, it "soars high, overcomes, and always gains the victory" over sin and the devil; and (3) the psalmist repeats the phrase because a "good song is worth singing twice."[61] Luther then brings the Christological point home:

> Whoever will, let him apply *these three points to the three-fold work of Christ*, in that He redeems us from the Law, from sin, and from death. This threefold redemption is

---

[60] *LW* 14:56.
[61] *LW* 14:82–83.

enumerated in Is. 9:4 and in 1 Cor. 15:55. As I have said,
however, the important thing is to realize that these words
are wholly spiritual and must be heard, sung, and understood by faith.[62]

Further, when David asks the Lord to "open the gates of righteousness for me" (Ps 118:19), Luther says that this is ultimately
"a heartfelt prayer for the Gospel and the kingdom of Christ" and
a request for "the removal of the burden of the Law of Moses, of
which Peter says (Acts 15:10) that neither our fathers nor we were
able to bear it."[63] Indeed, the "gates of righteousness" are the New
Testament churches where the gospel is preached to all.[64]

In sum, we notice here the comparison between Law and
Gospel, set within the reading of Psalm 118. Luther cites NT
passages for support, but still locates the Christological/Gospel
meaning in David's words. He does not draw on a *Quadriga* in his
commentary on the psalm and reorients the theological senses as
already textually present, but the elements of the fourfold sense are
still present in his "literal" reading: the literary and historical data,
the Christological/typological point, the emphasis on Christian
moral/spiritual response, and that longing for Christ's kingdom to
come to bear.

The Christian tradition was always keen on not allowing interpretation to terminate on mere exegetical or historical factoids, and
Luther was no different. Luther's insistence on Christ as the literal
sense was profoundly "practical"; that is, he saw Bible reading as
ultimately meant to transform believers through the work of Christ

---

[62] *LW* 14:83, emphasis mine.
[63] *LW* 14:90.
[64] *LW* 14:91.

and the Holy Spirit.[65] Indeed, as Robert Kolb aptly shows, Luther's ultimate aim in exegesis and preaching was to highlight justification by faith and imputed righteousness as a type of "metanarrative." As such,

> Because Luther believed that theology is a discipline that trains for practical application, he developed this hermeneutical approach to interpreting God's Word while being quite sensitive to the pastoral care it provided, particularly for anxious consciences. Faith receives a message from heaven so that "the law cannot make its demands on the troubled heart any longer; it has tortured and smothered us enough and must now give place to the gospel, which God's grace and mercy gives us."[66]

Because Christ is in all of Scripture, the literal sense points beyond mere words and historical facts, always ultimately pointing to Christ and the gospel as the hermeneutical key to understanding the biblical narrative. Biblical interpretation was not merely an academic exercise, but a pastoral/personal task centered around Christian living.

For Luther, then, there is no need for a multi-layered method of "senses" because the Law and gospel are brought into a dialectical

---

[65] For an introduction to Trinitarianism in Luther's reading of Scripture, see Christine Helmer, *The Trinity and Martin Luther*, rev. ed. (Bellingham, WA: Lexham, 2017). See also Mickey Mattox, "From Faith to the Text and Back Again: Martin Luther on the Trinity in the Old Testament," *Pro Ecclesia* 15/3 (2006): 281–303.

[66] Robert Kolb, *Luther and the Stories of God: Biblical Narratives as a Foundation for Christian Living* (Grand Rapids: Baker Academic, 2012), 21, quoting WA 36:22.

relationship centered on a singular textual meaning. This point reaches its rhetorical peak when Luther identifies Moses as a Christian in *The Last Words of David*.[67] The law and its commandments, then, can be lived out through love and good deeds only by the transforming power of the gospel.[68] To read God's Word is not to master a subject, but to encounter a Person.

Conclusion

It is sometimes assumed that the early church cared little for the literal sense. However, this brief survey reveals that this is not the case. Rather, premodern interpreters defaulted to the position that Scripture is divinely-inspired and contains the very words, wisdom, and power of God. And when certain teachers or groups of Christians left the literal sense behind, the church corrected these errors by reemphasizing the text and the history contained therein.

Origen of Alexandria, for all the (sometimes fair) critiques of his allegorical or spiritual readings, was deeply interested in Scripture's textual history and its intricate linguistic and theological patterns. John Chrysostom's allegorical or typological restraint is often welcomed by those otherwise suspicious of premodern interpretation, and yet he shows that the divine inspiration of Scripture requires more imagination than can be contained merely by textual studies or the human author's immediate intent. Hugh of Saint

---

[67] *LW* 15:299; WA 54:55. This is no doubt in part shaped by Luther's understanding of John 5:46 and Luke 24:27, wherein Jesus says that Moses wrote about him.

[68] Marsh, *Martin Luther on Reading the Bible as Christian Scripture*, 145–46.

Victor reminded his medieval counterparts that allegory is nothing without first understanding the way the words go, for in the history recorded in the text, we are able to marvel at God's providence in his dealings with mankind. In Martin Luther, we see an emphasis on the literal sense that in no way diminishes the spiritual significance of Scripture—divine inspiration helps us understand that the spiritual sense is always already contained in Scripture because Scripture is a divine book.

We cannot be taught by God if we do not first read the words he has given us. We must understand the intended meaning or significance of the text by first paying attention to context (both biblical and historical), genre, linguistic patterns, and a whole host of other important questions about the way the words go. There is no way to make sense of the following sensibilities—theological-Christological unity and communion with God—without first understanding the very words that make up Scripture's claims and commands.

Yet, premodern interpreters show us that the depth of Scripture requires more than this foundational sensibility. Scripture is not merely another book to be literarily criticized, historically terminated, or contextually reconstructed. No, Scripture is God's very Word to us. It is a book unlike any other—a book that is entirely truthful, authoritative, and transformative because of its divine origin. Abuses of this sensibility can blind us to the God who teaches us through his words, but an ancient understanding can show us its inextricable importance in understanding what God actually claims and commands in his Word.

3

How Does the Bible Fit Together?: Theological and Christological Unity

Scripture is God's revelation to his people and, thus, it is a fundamentally divine book.

As we saw in the previous chapter, premodern exegetes took Scripture's words seriously because of this very truth. And yet, they did not stop at the words themselves; they assumed that God's providential ordering of Scripture—indeed, his ordering of all of history itself—meant that the words did not terminate on mere word studies or historical facts. If Scripture is the revelation of God's providential ordering of all things, then interpreters should expect to find order and unity across the biblical canon. Most clearly, Christ stood at the center of the biblical narrative and its theological meaning.

Premodern exegetes across the board assumed a unity to God's revelation in Christ, because they first and foremost interpreted all of reality through the lens of God's creational order and providence. While the discussion around the development of the biblical canon is much larger than we can address here, it is fair to say that the early church assumed that a particular set of texts (with some diversity) was handed down from the apostles through the church under the guidance of the Holy Spirit. As such, it was generally assumed that no individual text lived on a proverbial island.

When seeking to find the theological and/or Christological unity of a given text, premodern exegetes wanted to understand what God was saying throughout time and space as the one who spoke through disparate authors in disparate times and places. In the event that a premodern exegete discussed "what Matthew or Paul meant," there was nonetheless a general assumption that Matthew's or Paul's words were pieces of a larger whole. One will rarely find an example of a premodern exegete singling out "Paul's theology" as though it could be meaningfully detached from "Matthew's" or "Peter's" theology. Even in early commentaries like Andrew of Caesarea's work on Revelation or John Chrysostom's sermons on particular books or passages, their notes and insights are flooded with cross-references and allusions to other biblical texts.

As we saw above, the modern impulse to granulate the biblical text into smaller, disjointed pieces is a different emphasis than the premodern exegetes operated from. Further, some of the historical-critical methodology of the twentieth century tended to dismiss the idea of the Bible's theological or canonical unity. While this emphasis has given us some helpful insights into the way the words go, it oftentimes resulted in a flattening of Scripture's theological subject matter and *telos*, treating the Bible like just another history book or work of literature. The premoderns defaulted to the assumption that the Bible was a unified revelation of God's acts in history, with Christ as the interpretive key.

Though there was always that theological thread that undergirded premodern interpretation, the Christological center of Scripture as the fulfillment of the Hebrew Scriptures/law was perhaps the most notable preoccupation. Irenaeus's claim that Christ is the key to the biblical kingly mosaic is not markedly different in sensibility from John Calvin's assertion that one must aim to find Christ in all of Scripture.[1] In that span from the second century (Justin) to the sixteenth (Calvin), the assumption that Christ unified the two Testaments was commonplace among premodern exegetes.

I will not belabor the various designations for this unifying thread, such as "allegory," "typology," "figural," and so forth; instead, I will allow these theologians to speak in their own ways and use their own terminology. So, regardless of how one adjudicates those designations, we will see in Irenaeus of Lyons, Athanasius of Alexandria, Thomas Aquinas, and John Calvin the sensibility among premodern exegetes to read Scripture through this theological-Christological thread in order to understand how Scripture fits together as divine revelation.

---

[1] This idea is drawn out in his commentary on John 5. See e.g., John Calvin, *The Gospel According to St John: 1–10, Calvin's New Testament Commentaries,* vol. 4, eds. David Torrance and Thomas Torrance, trans. T. H. L. Parker (Grand Rapids: Eerdmans, 1961), 139.

Irenaeus of Lyons

Irenaeus of Lyons, a second-century bishop of Lugdunum in Gaul (modern-day France), had a lasting influence on the Christian tradition through his so-called "rule of faith" or "truth" (κανών της αληθείας). This rule of faith was built upon an early Trinitarian formula:

> And this is the order of our faith, the foundation of [the] edifice and the support of [our] conduct: God, the Father, uncreated, uncontainable, invisible, one God, the Creator of all: this is the first article (κεφάλαιον) of our faith. And the second article: the Word of God, the Son of God, Christ Jesus our Lord, who was revealed by the prophets according to the nature of the economies of the Father, by whom all things were made, and who, in the last times, to recapitulate all things, became a man amongst men, visible and palpable, in order to abolish death, to demonstrate life, and to effect communion between God and man. And the third article: the Holy Spirit, through whom the prophets prophesied and the patriarchs learnt the things of God and the righteous were led in the path of righteousness, and who, in the last times, was poured out in a new fashion upon the human race renewing man, throughout the world, to God.[2]

---

[2] *Epid.* 6. English translations are from St. Irenaeus of Lyons, *On the Apostolic Preaching*, trans. John Behr (Crestwood, NY: St Vladimir's Seminary, 1997), 42–43.

For Irenaeus, the Christian life is shaped by the unified work of the Father, Son, and Holy Spirit. So, if Scripture is divine revelation—given by the Father, the Son and Word, and the Holy Spirit who inspires—then Scripture will be unified as well. This interpretive "hypothesis" or "key" (ὑπόθεσις) acted as an organizing principle for his biblical exegesis and theological deductions.

Irenaeus's main opponents are typically categorized under the umbrella of Gnosticism. Though Gnosticism took various forms, Irenaeus responded to those who denied the unity of God's revelation in Scripture by denying the authority of the OT writings and/or the apostolic witness in the NT.[3] Whereas some Gnostic groups claimed to have their own secret knowledge of divine revelation in non-canonical Gospels, Irenaeus asserted that God had given his revelation through the four canonical Gospels and other biblical writings that the apostles handed down.

In his *Against Heresies*, Irenaeus argues that the various portions of Scripture are like a mosaic made of "precious jewels" that, when arranged properly, reveals "a beautiful image of a king."[4] He charges the Valentinians, a Gnostic group, with obscuring the mosaic's true

---

[3] As mentioned above, space limits our engagement with canonical diversity in the early church, but in Irenaeus's major work, *Against Heresies*, he quotes or alludes to at least 21 of 27 NT books and particularly defends the authority of the four Gospels against the myriad "false" Gospels of the Gnostics. Further, he appears to utilize a taxonomy regarding Christian literature: (1) the prophets (authoritative/Scripture); (2) the apostles/letters (authoritative/Scripture); (3) the four Gospels/Jesus's words (authoritative/Scripture); and (4) other helpful writings (Clement; *Shepherd of Hermas*; his own writings).

[4] *AH* 1.8.1. English translations are from *The Ante-Nicene Fathers*, vol. 1, ed. Alexander Roberts, James Donaldson, and A. Cleveland Coxe,

image by interpreting it through the lens of either false scriptures or confusing parts of Scripture. In doing so, they "rearrange the gems, and so fit them together as to make them into the form of a dog or of a fox, and even that but poorly executed." They then "declare that this [image of the dog or fox] was the beautiful image of the king" and thus "deceive the ignorant who had no conception what a king's form was like, and persuade them that that miserable likeness of the fox was, in fact, the beautiful image of the king."[5]

This mosaic imagery is crucial for understanding Irenaeus's interpretive sensibilities. He makes a direct connection between Scripture's unity and its correct interpretation; however, more than that, this correct interpretation both points to and is driven by the "rule of faith/truth." Later in *Against Heresies*, he draws a clear line from the rule to good biblical interpretation. He argues that if a person reads the Scriptures via the rule—the triadic work of Father, Son, and Holy Spirit—he or she will see that "the entire Scriptures, the prophets, and the Gospels, can be clearly, unambiguously, and harmoniously understood by all."[6] However, if one follows the Gnostics and either adds to Scripture or elevates confusion over clarity, "no one will possess the rule of truth" but instead will find "various systems of truth, in mutual opposition to each other, and setting forth antagonistic doctrines."[7]

trans. Alexander Roberts and William Rambaut (New York: Christian Literature, 1885).

[5] *AH* 1.8.1.

[6] *AH* 2.27.2.

[7] *AH* 2.27.1. He says this particularly in the context of the parables, which can be more difficult to understand, especially without employing proper hermeneutical strategies.

In short, Irenaeus contends that Scripture is self-interpreting, such that the possibilities of the mosaic's final form are not endless. Indeed, if one does not find the king, one has ended up down a path that does not end in the unity of God's revelation. Why? Because if the Father, Son, and Holy Spirit are the "three articles" of the one "foundation" mentioned above, their unity grounds Scripture's unity. As Stephen Presley says, Irenaeus lays out a "theological networking of Scripture under the administration of God in three persons."[8]

As we move forward in church history to Athanasius, Thomas Aquinas, and Calvin, we should remember the importance of Irenaeus's articulation of the rule of faith for those who came after him. As Ayres has noted, Irenaeus "laid the foundations of the classical patristic exegesis of later centuries."[9] Of course, we should expect his contemporaries and even later interpreters to employ different emphases and come to different conclusions, but the rule of faith's insistence on the unity of God's revelation nonetheless ran through the premodern tradition.[10]

---

[8] Stephen O. Presley, "The *Demonstration* of Intertextuality in Irenaeus of Lyons," in *Intertextuality in the Second Century*, ed. D. Jeffrey Bingham and Clayton N. Jefford, The Bible in Ancient Christianity (Leiden: Brill, 2016), 197.

[9] Lewis Ayres, "Irenaeus vs. the Valentinians: Toward a Rethinking of Patristic Exegetical Origins," *Journal of Early Christian Studies* 23/2 (2015): 187.

[10] One could talk about the rule of faith in the plural, as there were various formulas that can be found implicitly and explicitly throughout the premodern tradition. However, as we will see, ruled readings were grounded in God as a truthful revelator.

Athanasius of Alexandria

Many of the figures covered in this book have extensive commentaries and homilies to mine for their interpretive approaches; however, fourth-century bishop Athanasius of Alexandria's extant works are largely theological and ethical treatises or letters. While there is no doubt he preached homilies with regularity as a local bishop, we have scant access to them.[11] Not only do we lack access to significant exegetical works, but a survey of the works we do have reveals that his approach varies based on the occasion or purpose of his writing.[12] The goal here, then, is not to argue for a strict Athanasian interpretive approach, but to highlight one of his core interpretive convictions: the "scope of Scripture" as an interpretive rule.

For Athanasius, the "scope" (σκοπός) does not merely relate generally to the whole biblical storyline, though that is part of it. More specifically, the "scope of Scripture" relates to the incarnation of the Son as the centerpoint of the biblical metanarrative. A common place to find this description can be found in the third book of his *Against the Arians*:

> Now the scope and character of Holy Scripture, as we have
> often said, is this,—it contains a double account of the
> Saviour; that He was ever God, and is the Son, being the

---

[11] One of the larger collections of biblical commentary once thought to belong to Athanasius were his expositions on the Psalter, though most scholars no longer consider them to be authentically Athanasian. See G. C. Stead, "St. Athanasius on the Psalms," *Vigiliae Christianae* 39/1 (1985): 65–78.

[12] For a helpful summary of the various proposals for Athanasius's exegetical "center," see James D. Ernest, *The Bible in Athanasius of Alexandria* (Atlanta: Society of Biblical Literature, 2010), 1–42.

Father's Word and Radiance and Wisdom; and that after-
wards for us He took flesh of a Virgin, Mary Bearer of
God, and was made man. And this scope is to be found
throughout inspired Scripture, as the Lord Himself has
said, "Search the Scriptures, for they are they which testify
of Me."[13]

Notice two convictions in this definition. First, the "scope" (and
"character") of Scripture reveals that the Son is both truly God
and truly man. This theological interpretive rule (later called "partitive exegesis") was crucial for defending the Nicene Creed (AD
325), which he sought to defend against various theologies he
deemed heretical.[14] Second, this scope is found throughout all of
Scripture because Jesus himself said this was the case in John 5:39.
Athanasius's interpretive approach to the scope of Scripture, then,
is centered on theological and Christological unity with respect
to the Son's incarnation and its influence on reading the biblical
metanarrative.

At the end of Book 2 of *Against the Arians*, Athanasius applies
this interpretive rule to Proverbs 8, a well-worn text in the early
church. Since Proverbs 8 talks about the "wisdom" of God and
the NT calls the Son "the wisdom of God" (e.g., 1 Cor 1:24), the
early church sought to understand the language of Prov 8:22—
"The LORD acquired [or 'created,' LXX] me at the beginning of

---

[13] *Con. Ar.* 3.29. English translations are from *The Nicene and Post-
Nicene Fathers*, vol. 4, ed. Philip Schaff and Henry Wace, trans. John
Henry Newman and Archibald T. Robertson (New York: Christian
Literature Company, 1892).

[14] For a similar partitive approach in the pro-Nicene period, see
Gregory of Nazianzus, *Or.* 29.

his creation, before his works of long ago"—as it relates to passages that seem to indicate the Son's existence before all of creation (e.g., John 1:1–3). How does one reconcile Scripture describing the Son both as "before all things were made" and as "made"? As Frances Young has rightly noted, this passage was consistently read as a reference to "the being who was the instrument through whom God created the universe," but the debate especially in the fourth-century Arian controversy was about the definition of ἔκτισεν ("he created").[15]

Athanasius says that "the heretics" falsely assume this means that the Son is a created being. But with the "scope" in view, one has to read these passages in light of the incarnation and with all of Scripture in mind. The heretics, he reasoned, were too myopic in their readings, taking passages out of context and thus offering poor interpretations of the text. If the Son is created, then he cannot also be the Creator as he is described elsewhere—this would mean Scripture has contradicted itself. As such, he offers an alternate reading with the scope of Scripture at the center.

First, Athanasius points out, "It is written, 'The Lord in Wisdom founded the earth' [Prov 3:19]; if then by Wisdom the earth is founded, how can He who founds be founded?"[16] Though he has already vigorously articulated a doctrine of the incarnation, he points out here that the immediate context of Proverbs already works against their proposal. With the presupposition that there is

---

[15] Frances Young, "Proverbs in Interpretation (2): Wisdom Personified; Fourth-Century Christian Readings: Assumptions and Debates," in *Reading Texts, Seeking Wisdom: Scripture and Theology*, ed. David F. Ford and Graham Stanton (London: Christian Student Movement, 2003), 103–6.

[16] *Con. Ar.* 2.73.

unity in God's revelation, Athanasius reasons that Prov 3:19 is not true if Prov 8:22 teaches the creation of Wisdom (the Son).

Second, Athanasius argues that the language in Proverbs might be better understood as the Son, the true Wisdom of God, being the one on whom all wisdom is founded: "[Paul] the Apostle also writes, 'Other foundation can no man lay than that is laid, which is Jesus Christ; but let every man take heed how he buildeth thereupon' [1 Cor 3:10–11]. And it must be that the foundation should be such as the things built on it . . ."[17] This comports with the assertion that the Son "took on flesh"—the uncreated one took on created flesh for us so that "according to His manhood He is rounded, that we, as precious stones, may admit of building upon Him, and may become a temple of the Holy Ghost who dwelleth in us."[18]

In summary, Athanasius's logic ultimately follows like this:

- The Son is God's eternal Wisdom. He did not "become wisdom" in time, for God cannot add wisdom to himself if he is eternally already perfect.
- Further, God created all things with and through the Son (Prov 3:19), making him the Creator, not a creature. Explanations for the Son as the first created divine being or the one who orders creation still insinuate that the Son is not eternal, and therefore is separated from the Father ontologically.
- Therefore, the language that may seem to indicate that the Son is created must relate to the incarnation when he put on flesh and became, as it were, a part of creation in

---

[17] *Con. Ar.* 2.74.
[18] *Con. Ar.* 2.74.

the economy of God. This fits with both the context of Proverbs and the larger biblical metanarrative about the identity of the Son.

As James Ernest points out, this "big picture" view of biblical interpretation is commonplace for Athanasius, in part because his opponents' proclivity for atomizing the text into particular words and phrases led to unbiblical conclusions.[19] The "scope of Scripture" acts as an interpretive move that best avoids making short-sighted interpretive decisions that challenge the unity of Christ's person and the Scriptures that unify around him.[20]

Like Irenaeus before him, Athanasius's sensibility for the theological and Christological unity of Scripture is the avenue through which he fights against the heresies of his day. The unity of God is at stake—the Father and Son must both be truly God if they are both described as eternal Creator—and the unity of Scripture is at stake—God's revelation cannot be contradictory if he is perfect. So, though we do not have large "commentaries" from Athanasius, we nonetheless see his theological deductions being rooted in biblical interpretation. Further, like Irenaeus, this is more than a theological debate—the heretical conclusions of his opponents lead them to deny the true God presented in Scripture, and thus their interpretive method is a worship issue.

---

[19] Ernest, *The Bible in Athanasius of Alexandria*, 171–72.

[20] Interestingly, he already challenged the inconsistency of the "literal" and "allegorical" interpretive moves of these heretics in *Con. Ar.* 2.46: "When Scripture says, 'Wisdom built her a house, she set it upon seven pillars' [Prov 9:1], [they] understand 'house' allegorically, but [they] take 'He created' as it stands ["literally"], and [they] fasten on it the idea of creature . . ."

Thomas Aquinas

Widely considered among the greatest theologian-philosophers in history, the thirteenth-century friar Thomas Aquinas joined the Victorines and others in recovering the importance of the literal sense in the medieval period. As we saw in chapter 1, Aquinas viewed the literal sense—the "words and things" in the text—as the foundation of all biblical interpretation. So, the "way the words go" was the controlling factor for applying his threefold division of the spiritual sense: (1) allegorical (when the Old signifies the New), (2) moral (what we ought to do), and (3) anagogical (what relates to eternal glory).[21] Simply put, one could not expect to rightly read Scripture in any spiritual sense without a proper understanding of the literal. In this way, Aquinas resonated with—and was indeed influenced by—the sensibilities of the Christian tradition that preceded him.

Aquinas's writings are so voluminous and detailed that it is tempting to cite him as an example in each of the three sensibilities covered in this book; however, I have settled on highlighting his articulation of the unity of Scripture due to his insights on the theological and Christological basis for this unity. In particular, as Michael Dauphinais notes, Aquinas presents the OT and NT as "Old and New Laws" that relate as "the imperfect and the perfect."[22] This imperfect-perfect relationship is best understood as a move from immature to mature, because "the Old Law was intrinsically

---

[21] *ST* I, q. 1, a. 9.

[22] Michael Dauphinais, "The Place of Christ and the Biblical Narrative in Aquinas's Theology," in *Thomas Aquinas: Biblical Theologian*, ed. Roger Nutt and Michael Dauphinais (Steubenville, OH: Emmaus Academic, 2021), 19.

ordered to the rejection of idols, to the right worship of God, and to its fulfillment in Christ."[23] Put another way, the OT offers God's commands or precepts; the NT shows the incarnation's ultimate revelation of God in Christ, the cause and motivation of Christian faith. For example, in a lecture on Scripture, Aquinas notes that the NT "is ordered to eternal life, not only by precepts, but through the gifts of grace . . ."[24] Thus, the OT is valuable insofar as it is God's revelation, but God's revelation in the biblical narrative finds its perfection or maturity in the revelation of the Son. As Dauphinais summarizes, "Christ himself offers in all that he does the definitive meaning of both the Old and New Laws. The Incarnation thus does not serve merely as a datum of revelation, but as the historical disclosure of saving truth."[25]

Aquinas's commentary on Psalm 8 is a clear example of this move from imperfect to perfect. He starts by highlighting that "the psalmist wonders at the divine excellence" before explaining "two kinds of people who follow the natural and correct impulses: the simple and the wise."[26] The rest of the psalm, first, lays out how humanity can live as rightly human in light of God's grace. For example, the psalmist answers the question "what is man?" in three

---

[23] Dauphinais, "The Place of Christ," 20; see *ST* I-II, q. 102, a.3, ad 1.

[24] *Hic Est Lib.* English translation is from St. Thomas Aquinas, *Commentary on Psalms, Rigans Montes, Hic Est Liber,* trans. John R. Gilhooly, Albert Marie Surmanski, and Maria Veritas Marks (Steubenville, OH: Emmaus Academic, 2021). Gilhooly translated *Hic Est Lib.*

[25] Dauphinais, "The Place of Christ," 19.

[26] *Comm. Pss.* 52–53. English translation is from St. Thomas Aquinas, *Commentary on Psalms, Rigans Montes, Hic Est Liber,* trans. John R. Gilhooly, Albert Marie Surmanski, and Maria Veritas Marks (Steubenville, OH: Emmaus Academic, 2021). Surmanski and Marks translated *Comm. Pss.*

ways: first, the psalm is shaped so that worship of God is the foundation by showing humanity's place below God; second, "by comparison with the first man" in saying, "you have crowned him with glory and honor"; and third, "by comparison with those things which are under man" in saying, "you have set him over the works of your hands."[27] Aquinas continues this line of thinking throughout the psalm, noting God's gratuitous grace toward mankind, and asserting that mankind's dignity and worth is wrapped up in God's willingness to create, enlighten, and come alongside humanity.

Aquinas then comes back around and re-reads the passage Christologically, since "the favors of grace" toward humanity listed in the passage are "enumerated" in "all the mysteries of Christ."[28] For example, "what is man?" refers to the incarnation, in which the Son visited humanity in general and a human nature/body in particular. Further, "you have set him over the works of your hands" and "you have subjected all things under his feet" refers to humanity's general dignity, but are perfected in Christ ascension and place of judgment at the right hand of God.[29] For Aquinas, then, Psalm 8 reflects the commands and precepts of the "Old Law"—that is, God's desire for humanity—and their *telos* found Christ's "New Law"—that is, his fulfillment of humanity's *telos* in the incarnation.

John Calvin

John Calvin, the sixteenth-century French pastor and theologian, rivals Luther in terms of lasting Reformation influence. He was

---

[27] *Comm. Pss.* 55.
[28] *Comm. Pss.* 56.
[29] *Comm. Pss.* 56.

acquainted with the interpretive methods and approaches of other Reformers, including Luther, Martin Bucer, and Ulrich Zwingli, though not uncritical of their approaches.[30] Further, he was self-consciously a theologian in the lineage of the early church, especially Augustine, as many of the Reformers were.

That said, though he shares this sensibility of biblical unity with major voices in the Christian tradition, Calvin's approach to the theological and Christological unity of Scripture has its own flavor. In particular, he employed a type of redemptive-historical approach that often related the OT and NT as a movement from promise to fulfillment. When Calvin speaks in his writings about interpretation and the unity of Scripture, a few convictions consistently stand out.

First, he saw Scripture as divinely-inspired and, thus, authoritative and interconnected. Second, the unity of Scripture was demonstrated by clear textual connections. For example, when speaking on the early church's approach to interpretation, he compares Augustine and Chrysostom. Though Calvin is perhaps more influenced by Augustine than any other ancient figure, he nonetheless says that Augustine's allegorical moves can be "too sly" and thus "less firm and solid"; Chrysostom, however, is a better model because he tethers himself to "the germane sense of Scripture" without "contorting the simple sense of the words."[31] Third, the primary way to read Scripture rightly and in light of the first two convictions is through the Spirit's illumination. We see these convictions

---

[30] *CR* 38.404–39.36.

[31] I owe Richard C. Gamble for this comparison in "*Brevitas et Facilitas*: Toward an Understanding of Calvin's Hermeneutic," *Westminster Theological Journal* 47 (1985): 8–9.

on display in his brief commentary on 2 Cor 3:6–17, which we have already seen as an important text throughout the Christian tradition in figures like Origen and Augustine.[32]

He begins by explaining his view on Paul's use of "letter" and "Spirit":

> there is no doubt that by the letter he meant the Old Testament, as by the word Spirit he means the gospel; for, when he calls himself a minister of the new covenant, he also adds immediately that he is a minister of the Spirit; and it is in this connection that he contrasts the letter with the Spirit.[33]

More specifically, "Paul calls the law *letter* because in itself it is dead preaching; and he calls the gospel 'Spirit,' because its ministry is alive and makes alive."[34] This is an important distinction for Calvin, because he sees Paul as using these two terms in direct contrast: when Paul compares letter and Spirit, he is specifically highlighting "the nature of the law" that does not penetrate "beyond the ear" versus "the nature of the gospel to teach spiritually" through "the grace of Christ."[35] Put succinctly, the function of the law was chis-

---

[32] English translations are from *Calvin: Commentaries*, ed. and trans. Joseph Haroutunian and Louise Pettibone Smith (Philadelphia: Westminster, 1958). Calvin interacts with the interpretations of "Origen and others" on this text.

[33] Calvin, *Commentaries*, 107.

[34] Calvin, 108, emphasis original.

[35] Calvin, 108. He is quick to note that "Even the gospel itself is not always *Spirit*," so the terms must be defined this way only when Paul himself compares the way people think of or use the law and the gospel.

eled on stones and therefore breakable; the function of the gospel is
given by the Spirit and therefore unbreakable.[36]

For Calvin, then, Origen's interpretation of letter/Spirit as
literal/allegorical is dangerous because it leads to some into believing that "Scripture is not only useless but even harmful unless it
is turned into elaborate allegories."[37] Instead, Calvin insists, "God
has conferred great honor upon the law, which is as nothing in
comparison with the gospel. . . . So he argues from the *lesser* to
the *greater*, and presents the glory of the gospel as all the more
magnificent since it is far superior to the law."[38] Calvin's concern
with "allegory" in this sense is a concern for interpretations that
go beyond what the Bible warrants. When running off to allegory,
Calvin contends, one misses that the letter/law is itself instituted by
God and therefore good. In fact, neither law nor gospel themselves
condemn people; rather, people condemn themselves when their
confidence is misplaced. Confidence in the law leads to death and
condemnation because it offers no hope of a cure for breaking it;
confidence in the gospel leads to life because Christ, the hope of
eternal life, is found there.[39]

Calvin rounds out his view on the theological and Christological
unity of Scripture via Paul's commentary on Israel's "blindness":

> If the Jews seek Christ in the law, God's truth will appear
> to them clearly; while they continue to seek wisdom
> without Christ, they shall lose their way in darkness and

---

[36] Calvin, 109.
[37] Calvin, 108.
[38] Calvin, 108–9, emphasis mine.
[39] Calvin, 109–10.

never arrive at the true meaning of the law. What is said
of the law applies to the whole of Scripture: when it is not
directed toward Christ as its one aim, it is tortured badly
and twisted.[40]

Again, Calvin does not dismiss the law as entirely useless but argues
that it must be understood in light of Christ's fulfillment of it.
Indeed, Paul is commending the law just as David does in the psalter; however, "When Christ gives life to the law, David's praises
apply to it; when Christ is taken away, the law is altogether as Paul
describes it. Therefore, Christ is the life of the law."[41] So Israel's
confidence in the law itself misses the point because they have confidence in a set of breakable tablets. But when one listens to "the
Spirit of the Lord," he listens to and receives the grace of Christ.

In his short exposition on 2 Cor 3:6–17, Calvin reveals a great
deal about his approach to the unity of Scripture. In Paul, he sees
someone who holds together the unity of the OT and NT by highlighting the goodness of the law insofar as its *telos* is Christ. There
was no need for what Calvin deems as problematic allegorizing;
instead, he tracked along with Chrysostom once again, asserting
that Paul's "allegory" in Galatians 4 was admissible because it was
(1) consistent with the plain or literal meaning and (2) reasonable
based on Paul's broader argument about slavery and freedom.[42] For
Calvin, then, Scripture's unity is built upon a redemptive-historical

---

[40] Calvin, 112.

[41] Calvin, 112–13.

[42] John Calvin, *Commentaries on the Epistle of Paul to the Galatians
and Ephesians*, trans. William Pringle, Calvin Translation Society (Grand
Rapids: Baker, 1996), 134–36.

movement from law to gospel, centered on Christ, and illuminated
by the Spirit. While the nuances are obvious, he shared the same
sensibility of other premoderns before him, who saw Scripture as a
unified witness to Christ.

Conclusion

Developing a sensibility for the theological-Christological unity of
Scripture is not a one-way ticket to ignoring the way the words go.
Quite the opposite! Irenaeus of Lyons shows us that Christ as the
hermeneutical key to Scripture both remains faithful to his own
claims about being the center of Scripture (Luke 24:44; John 5:46;
8:56) and also highlights the larger divine providence in inspir-
ing a certain set of texts over and against others. Athanasius of
Alexandria continues this rule of faith, showing that a sensibility
about the theological-Christological unity of Scripture helps clarify
the meaning of texts that are not as clear as others. Aquinas builds
on this foundation, putting together a more structured "method"
of when a spiritual reading is within the bounds of the way the
words go. Calvin reminds us that with the Spirit, we are all able to
understand Scripture's unified witness to Christ as we read the very
words of God in the text.

This sensibility is in many ways a linchpin for faithful interpretation of Scripture. The way the words go is the foundation,
but we cannot stop there. Indeed, premodern interpreters are
quick to point out that Israel rejected their Messiah in part because
they could not move past the literal sense to seeing Christ in their
Scriptures. Scripture tells us that it fits together in a certain way
by being thoroughly self-referential, pointing back to figures and
events that have come before and looking ahead to figures and

events that keep the story going. There is no doubt that this sensibility can become unhinged in such a way that interpreters could make Scripture say anything with just a little dash of Jesus on top, but faithful interpreters from the past show us how to properly restrain our spiritual readings by the text itself.

4

How Then Should We Live?: Personal and Ecclesial Communion with God

Scripture is meant to transform us.

When one considers the creeds and the theological debates of the early church, it might be easy to assume that the early church was much more concerned with lists of cold doctrinal facts than the warmth of loving and following the risen Lord. However, theological eggheadedness was far from the premoderns' minds. As we saw in the previous chapter, biblical interpretation led to doxology and praxis, in large part because Scripture shaped what one believed, how one lived, and one's place in the church both locally and universally.

As with every sensibility we have discussed, there was at times sharp diversity on how one applied the biblical text to the personal and moral communal life. Throughout most of the Christian tradition, applications of this sensibility ranged from the Desert Fathers who lived in entire isolation as a form of obedience and service to the Lord, to others who served as bishops in densely-populated metropolises. In general, though, the premodern church was not nearly as individualistic as some Christians can be—biblical interpretation was not merely a personal opinion, but shaped communal life. In fact, even the ascetics who lived in isolation did so with the goal of serving the church, and many would hold audiences with bishops and other members of the Christian community to offer wisdom based off their life of contemplation.

Further, those engaging in the nuances of theological debate saw worship as a central component. A clear example is Athanasius's defense of Nicaea against Arianism and similar theological groups who denied the Son's true divinity. For Athanasius, confessing the Son's true divinity was not merely a definitional or grammatical issue (though it was), but it was ultimately a worship issue. All of creation worships the Son, he said, because the Son is truly divine and thus worthy of worship.[1] If Jesus is merely a creature like us, he is not worthy of our worship and we would have to fundamentally reorder our personal devotion and the church's liturgy. When the Nicene Creed says that the Son is "true God of true God," for example, this is a statement about what the Bible teaches and what churches should confess in worship. While some may tend to separate "personal faith" from corporate ecclesial belief and practice, premoderns tended to view them as deeply intertwined.

---

[1] *Con. Ar.* 2.20.

For example, if one denied the church's orthodox teaching on the Trinity, this false belief was both a sign of personal false belief or idolatry and a sign that one has left the body of Christ.

Finally, premodern exegetes were heavenly-minded. As premodern exegetes read the text, drew out unifying theological/Christological threads, and considered how they should live, the eschatological question was not far behind. This eschatological impulse was not primarily built around mere debates like the timing of a "rapture" or the date when Jesus would return (though these questions arose at times); rather, their eschatological outlook was primarily centered on eternal hope and rest in light of present suffering and political uncertainty, the spiritual realities of personal and ecclesial life, and the contemplation of how heavenly or immaterial realities touch down in the material world in myriad ways. Ultimately, they knew the Scriptures provided hope—and this conviction was not a detached theological idea, but central to their exegetical conclusions and insights.

Some have called this heavenly-mindedness the "beatific vision" or the "anagogical sense," and whether a figure used these terms or not, this idea of seeing God "face-to-face," as it were, is the *telos* of the moral life. Rather than viewing history merely as a way to describe the linear movement of history from some beginning point toward an end point, premoderns were more predisposed to see history under the umbrella of God's transcendent providence and eternity. While a linear understanding of history was not a foreign concept by any means, it was nonetheless understood against the backdrop of divine timelessness. This sensibility, then, views reality itself and the unfolding of history we observe as containing types, figures, and/or signs. For sure, apocalyptic or eschatological realities contain some sort of linear *telos* in new creation; however,

premodern exegetes also understood them to contain present spiritual realities and immediate hope. The ultimate hope for premoderns was not merely a longing for heaven or new creation, though it
involved this element; it was also a wider understanding of history
and human experience that viewed these apocalyptic or eschatological realities as already available through God's transcendent providence. And one day, of course, believers will have a full beatific
vision and truly see God "face-to-face."

In Justin Martyr, Augustine of Hippo, John of Damascus, and
William Tyndale, we will see the consistent sensibility among premodern Christians that Scripture's truths must come to bear in the
personal and ecclesial life of God's people with an end goal of eternal communion with God.

Justin Martyr

Second-century apologist Justin Martyr began his religious and
intellectual life with a deep affinity for Greco-Roman philosophy,
particularly forms of Platonism that were popular in his day. As he
recalls, Platonic philosophy "added wings to my mind [such that] I
fully expected immediately to gaze upon God."[2] However, Martyr
tells a story about meeting a Christian and hearing the gospel for
the first time: "My spirit was immediately set on fire, and an affec-
tion for the Prophets and for those who are friends of Christ took

---

[2] *Dial.* 2. English translations of the two *Apologies* and *Dialogue with
Trypho* are from Saint Justin Martyr, *The First Apology, The Second Apology,
Dialogue with Trypho, Exhortation to the Greeks, Discourse to the Greeks, The
Monarchy or Rule of God*, The Fathers of the Church vol. 6, trans. Thomas
B. Falls (Washington, DC: Catholic University of America, 1948).

hold of me; while pondering on his words, I discovered that this was the only sure and useful philosophy."[3] As was common with many premodern Christian theologians, his view of Christ shaped his reading of Scripture as a whole. In particular, Christ as the *Logos* or "Word" had massive implications for his interpretive approach and how it worked out in his life and ministry.

His two *Apologies* (*First Apology* and *Second Apology*) and *Dialogue with Trypho* contain lucid examples of his Christology. The *Apologies* are aimed at a Greek audience, positing Christ in Scripture as the fulfillment of ancient philosophies; however, in the *Dialogue* his interlocuter is a Jewish man named Trypho, so his concern is more focused on Christ as the direct referent of Scripture.[4] His conversion led him to argue that both the Jews and the Greeks erred in their views of the world—only Christianity is the "sure and useful philosophy."

In his *Apologies*, Martyr notably used Stoic and Platonic ideas to build an apologetic for Christ from John 1: the same *Logos* the Greeks ("pagans") spoke of appeared in the person of Jesus Christ ("the Word"). For example, he notes that Greek heroes such as Mercury ("the announcing word of God"), Jupiter's sons ("who suffered"), and Perseus ("born of a virgin") are comparable to Jesus, but "as we have already proved . . . He is their superior."[5] Here, Martyr elevates Jesus higher than the Greek philosophies by personifying the *Logos* and painting him as the true and better *Logos*. He spoke in other places about the unique relationship between the Father and Son:

---

[3] *Dial.* 7.
[4] Behr, *The Way to Nicaea*, 94–96.
[5] *1 Apol.* 22.

No proper name has been bestowed upon God, the Father of all, since He is unbegotten. . . . But His Son, who alone is properly called Son, the Word, who was with Him [God the Father] and was begotten before all things, when in the beginning He [God, the Father] created and arranged all things through him [the Son].[6]

Concerning the Jewish people, Martyr tells Trypho that Israel's Scriptures are "not yours, but ours."[7] Why? "If your ears were not so dull, or your hearts so hardened, you would see that the words refer to our Jesus."[8] As many of the other early Christian apologists, Martyr saw that Israel's God was always closely tied to his *Logos*—inseparable from the Father as light from the sun—which has now been seen in Jesus.[9]

All of this "philosophy" talk sounds highly academic for a chapter on personal and ecclesial communion with God, but this was not how premoderns often viewed philosophy. Philosophy was not a mere academic discipline, but rather a whole way of living. The quest for the "true" philosophy was connected to the quest for the good life. Philosophy was, then, a means to an end—finding meaning and beauty in the world. For Martyr, the true philosophy—the true good life—was found in Christ and his teachings, whom the Greeks mocked and the Jews rejected.

For example, in the midst of intense persecution and accusations of debauchery from the Greco-Roman authorities, Martyr appealed to the Sermon on the Mount as a model for Christian

---

[6] *2 Apol.* 6.
[7] *Dial.* 29.
[8] *Dial.* 33.
[9] *Dial.* 128–29.

living and as a defense for Christian religious freedom. Citing several passages from Matthew 5, Martyr asserts to the Roman emperor that Jesus "taught us that we should be patient, and be willing to submit to everyone, and never give way to anger."[10] In fact, Martyr argues, Christian converts in Rome have become more morally upright either post-conversion or at least in light of watching their Christian neighbors' lives.[11] Martyr is so convinced that Scripture like the Sermon transforms people that he says, citing Matt 7:21–23, "May they who are not found living according to His teachings know that they are not Christians, even though they profess with their tongues the teaching of Christ."[12] Further, Christian persecution is unwarranted because the Scriptures also teach submission to civil authorities (Matt 22:20–21; Luke 12:48). For Martyr, then, the Sermon provides a model for Christian living, and true Christians can be distinguished by comparing their works to the Sermon's commands.

Martyr comes back to this point in his *Dialogue with Trypho*. Here again he quotes Matthew 7 to defend Trypho's claim that some Christians claim there is no harm in eating meat sacrificed to idols. Anyone who claims Christ but openly disobeys him is "outside of our communion, for we know them for what they are, impious atheists and wicked sinners, men who profess Jesus with their lips, but do not worship Him in their hearts."[13] In both instances—whether arguing against the Greeks or the Jews—Martyr cannot see a distinction between right reading of Scripture and right living.

---

[10] *1 Apol.* 16.
[11] *1 Apol.* 16.
[12] *1 Apol.* 16.
[13] *Dial.* 35.

Martyr saw Christianity as the true and better philosophy
because it made better sense of reality, morality, and eternity than
any story in Greco-Roman philosophy or the Jewish story. In particular, Martyr constantly returned to the point that Scripture calls
Christians to confess Christ as a better hope than the Greek systems
and as the fulfillment of the Jewish hope in the prophets and writings. Far from a mere hermeneutical debate, Martyr was adamant
that Scripture, read rightly, transformed its readers.

Augustine of Hippo

As mentioned in a previous chapter, Augustine's writings and sermons span his ministry, are a product of his own self-conscious
autobiographical journey as a Christian and bishop, involve myriad
topics and biblical passages, and are set within the context of the
church's developing theological and rhetorical culture; as such, his
exegetical method is difficult to define.[14] Further, we should note
once again that for many of these early premodern interpreters,
a hard-and-fast "method" was often not the goal or the primary
intent of exegesis. Even his aforementioned groundbreaking theory of semiotics ("things" and "signs") was rigorous and important to his interpretive practice, but it was not ultimately aimed
at mere interpretive methodology. Augustine explicitly notes that
the "signs" are important primarily because they remind us that

---

[14] As Karla Pollman points out, the feeling that there are "multiple
Augustines" is perhaps exacerbated by the fact that Augustine is so autobiographical and conscious of his contexts. See Karla Pollman, "*Alium sub
meo nomine*: Augustine between His Own Self-Fashioning and His Later
Reception," *Zeitschrift für Antikes Christentum* 14 (2010): 409–24.

Scripture speaks spiritually beyond the mere words and to the heart of the reader/hearer, that he or she may grow in wisdom. Put another way, Scripture points to the dual loves (*caritas*): love God and love others. In sum, then, Augustine's interpretive practice(s) is carefully crafted and yet ultimately not about mere method but about virtuous Christian living.

So, the various ways Augustine interpreted Scripture focused not only on the theological-Christological unity, but also on spiritual formation. Scripture's words are God's words, and so the Spirit's "intention" exceeds the intention of the human authors.[15] One cannot simply read the text "literally" and then move on to understand its unity—one must also allow the text to penetrate his or her heart. Indeed, it is impossible to talk about Augustine's life and ministry without being drawn toward his deep love for God in his *Confessions*, an autobiography written at the end of the fourth century about his radical conversion to Christianity. As Matthew Levering points out, "Augustine states [in his *Retractions*] that his reason for writing his *Confessions* . . . was to move the mind—his own and others'—toward God in love."[16] So, throughout the work, Augustine includes countless passages from the OT and NT to encourage Christian worship.

Augustine famously opens the *Confessions* with the exclamation that "you [God] have made us for yourself, and our heart is restless until it rests in you."[17] This thesis statement pervades the

---

[15] See e.g., *De Doc.* 2.5.6 and 3.7.11.

[16] Matthew Levering, *The Theology of Augustine: An Introductory Guide to His Most Important Works* (Grand Rapids: Baker Academic, 2013), 89; see *Retr.* 32.1.

[17] *Conf.* 1.1.1. English translations are from Saint Augustine, *Confessions: A New Translation by Henry Chadwick* (Oxford: Oxford

work as he navigates his own spiritual journey and reflects on his interactions with various philosophies, theologies, and moral values. At the end of *Confessions*, he draws on the book of Genesis as the linchpin for understanding the moral and ecclesial life of the Christian.

God as the Creator in Genesis 1–2 is the centering doctrine for Augustine when reflecting on our relationship to him: "Your creation has its being from the fullness of your goodness. . . . From you, the One, the supreme Good, they have being and are all 'very good' (Gen. 1:31)."[18] Of course, as the biblical story goes, mankind sinned and turned away from the light of God and toward darkness. Because God did not need us and chose to create us anyway "from the fullness of [his] goodness," he does the work of restoring us: "When scripture says your Spirit rests on people (Isa. 11:2), it means that the Spirit makes them rest on himself."[19] Drawing on Isaiah and numerous psalms, Augustine shows that God's work in restoring mankind leads to perfection: "more and more to live by the fount of life, to see light in his light (Ps. 35:10), and to become perfect, radiant with light, and in complete happiness."[20] This does not mean, of course, that man becomes perfect in the same way that God is perfect; rather, his view of "perfection" is a habit of pursuing virtue by the Spirit in order to live righteously in this life in light of God's perfection.[21] Indeed, the Spirit hovered over the waters at creation (Gen 1:2), and therefore, "we may lift up our heart and

---

University, 1991).

[18] *Conf.* 13.2.2.
[19] *Conf.* 13.4.5.
[20] *Conf.* 13.4.5.
[21] See 1.8.18.

hold it to you, where your Spirit is 'borne above the waters', and we come to the supereminent resting-place when our soul has passed over 'the waters that are without substance' (Ps. 123:5)."[22]

This triune God who created all things can work through Christ in the Spirit to bring us back to our intended state as worshippers of our Creator—we can be on the road to perfection once again. In his sermon on the Sermon on the Mount, Augustine similarly draws on the idea of perfection being the end goal of the Christian life. For Augustine, the Beatitudes' virtues are prerequisites for those who wish live in God's "most peaceful and orderly kingdom."[23]

We saw above that Augustine draws on Isaiah 11 to explain the Holy Spirit's work in restoring mankind to "perfection," and he draws on it again here. He sees the sevenfold operation of the Holy Spirit in Isa 11:2–3 as a parallel to the seven beatitudes that lead to the eighth—"Blessed are those who are persecuted because of righteousness, for the kingdom of heaven is theirs" (Matt 5:10)[24]. Augustine sees this eighth beatitude as the completion of the seven beatitudes and a return to the promise of the first beatitude—"for the kingdom of heaven is theirs" (Matt 5:3).[25]

Augustine then contemplates the Beatitudes' relationship to the sevenfold operation of the Spirit in Isa 11:2–3: "So it seems to

---

[22] *Conf.* 13.7.8.

[23] *Serm. Dom. Mont.* 1.19. My translation of "regno pacatissimo et ordinatissimo." All translations from *Serm. Dom. Mont.* are mine, sourced from the Latin text in PL 34:1229–1308.

[24] This sevenfold description is found in the LXX.

[25] *Serm. Dom. Mont.* 1.3.10: "The eighth returns, as it were, to the start . . . the eighth clarifies and demonstrates what is perfect . . ." ("Octava tamquam ad caput redit . . . nam octava clarificat, et quod perfectum est demonstrat . . .").

me that the sevenfold operation of the Holy Spirit, of which Isaiah speaks, corresponds to these stages and maxims."[26] As he explains, Isaiah begins with wisdom and the virtues descend from there; in Jesus's sermon, the Beatitudes start with the fear of the Lord and ascend toward wisdom. He then draws on Prov 9:10: "Thus it is said, *Blessed are the poor in spirit, for theirs is the kingdom of heaven* as if it were said, *The fear of the Lord is the beginning of wisdom.*"[27] Wisdom and the fear of the Lord are thus interconnected. The connection between Matthew 5 and Isaiah 11 becomes clear: the gifts listed in the sevenfold operation of the Holy Spirit are attainable through pursuing the virtues found in Jesus's words in the Sermon. Wisdom is the end goal for those who seek the kingdom of God.

This all comes to fruition at Pentecost (Acts 2):

> On which day the Holy Spirit was sent, by whom we are led into the kingdom of heaven, and receive an inheritance, and are comforted, and are fed, and obtain mercy, and are cleansed, and made peacemakers, and being thus perfected, we endure all troubles brought upon us externally for the sake of truth and righteousness.[28]

---

[26] *Serm. Dom. Mont.* 1.4.11. "Videtur ergo mihi etiam septiformis operatio Spiritus Sancti, de qua Isaias loquitur, his gradibus sententiisque congruere."

[27] *Serm. Dom. Mont.* 1.4.12. "Sic itaque dictum est: *Beati pauperes spiritu, quoniam ipsorum est regnum caelorum*, tamquam diceretur: *Initium sapientiae timor Domini.*"

[28] "Quo die missus est Spiritus Sanctus, quo in regnum caelorum ducimur et haereditatem accipimus et consolamur et pascimur et misericordiam consequimur et mundamur et pacificamur. Atque ita perfecti omnesextrinsecus illatas molestias pro veritate et iustitia sustinemus."

As we mentioned above, Augustine's interpretation seeks to ultimately reach the heart of the believer. Notice that Augustine does not merely expound upon the beatitudes; he also grounds it in the larger biblical witness about the wisdom God seeks to produce in his people. What Isaiah preached then is what Jesus preached later. And now, on the other side of Pentecost, Christians partake in these promises and begin to learn the habit of contemplating on the God who made and saved them. For Augustine, the *visio dei* ("vision of God") was the pinnacle of the *frui Deo* ("enjoyment of God"). This vision is ultimately not merely for the individual, but for the baptized body of Christ in the church.

John of Damascus

Born around AD 657–676, John of Damascus was an influential monk and priest known for his views on the benefit of icons,[29] his writings against Islam,[30] and hymn-writing. *The Orthodox Faith* is one of his towering works which, as Andrew Louth notes, "remains

---

[29] See St John of Damascus, *Three Treatises on the Divine Images*, trans. Andrew Louth (Crestwood, NY: SVS, 2003).

[30] For example, John surmised that the "heresy" of Islam had its roots in Arianism: "From that time to the present a false prophet named Mohammed has appeared in their midst. This man, after having chanced upon the Old and New Testaments and likewise, it seems, having conversed with an Arian monk, devised his own heresy. Then, having insinuated himself into the good graces of the people by a show of seeming piety, he gave out that a certain book had been sent down to him from heaven," in *Haer.* 101. English translations of *Haer.* and *De Fide* are from St. John of Damascus, *Writings*, trans. Frederic H. Chase, Jr. (Washington DC: Catholic University of America, 1958). Thanks to Matthew Bennett for pointing out this citation.

an incomparable *summa* of theology and an indispensable aid to the study of the Greek Christian tradition," given his reliance on figures such as the Cappadocians, Athanasius of Alexandria, Maximus Confessor, and Chrysostom.[31] After the first two books tackle theological subjects such as the doctrines of God and creation, Books III and IV turn to the question of humanity and our salvation. His teachings on salvation are smattered with biblical references, so I will simply lay out a summary and highlight some of the biblical texts that John draws on.

He starts the third book with a stark statement about the fall of mankind: "And so, man succumbed to the assault of the demon, the author of evil; he failed to keep the Creator's commandment and was stripped of grace and deprived of that familiarity which he had enjoyed with God."[32] God's way of destroying sin in mankind was evident in the OT as God "schooled" and "exhorted" mankind toward a return to blessedness via suffering, judgment, divine appearances, and the Law and Prophets—but "the most fitting solution for this most difficult problem" was the incarnation of the Son.[33] The fourth book then reflects on the incarnation's implications for mankind, namely, "The Son of God became man in order that He might again grace man as He had when He made him."[34]

Through faith and baptism, John asserts that mankind can be truly restored to its intended purpose as obedient image-bearers. John defines faith in a two-fold manner: (1) "'faith cometh by

---

[31] St. John of Damascus, *Writings*, xxxv.
[32] *De Fide* 3.1.
[33] *De Fide* 3.1.
[34] *De Fide* 4.4.

hearing' [Rom 10:17], for, when we hear the sacred Scriptures, we believe in the teaching of the Holy [Spirit]" and (2) "there is a faith 'which is the substance of things to be hoped for, the evidence of things that appear not' [Heb 11:1]."[35] In summary, says John, "The first kind of faith comes from our faculty of judgment, whereas the second is one of the gifts of the Spirit."[36] Baptism and faith, then, make us "spiritual Israelites and a people of God."[37]

John then exhorts those who walk in faith to look at "the honorable cross," which was "of all things [he did during his earthly ministry] the most wonderful."[38] The cross is central because, as John notes, it is foolishness to the world and not perceivable by those without the Spirit (1 Cor 1:18; 2:14–15). This is not the case for believers:

> If, however, one is guided by faith and concludes to the goodness, omnipotence, truth, wisdom, and justice of the Godhead, then he will find all things to be smooth and even and the road straight. Without faith it is impossible to be saved [Heb 11:6], since by faith all things endure, both human and spiritual. . . . By the cross all things have been set aright. 'For all we who are baptized in Christ,' says the Apostle, 'are baptized in his death' [Rom 6:3] and 'as many of us as have been baptized in Christ have put on Christ' [Gal 3:27] . . .[39]

---

[35] *De Fide* 4.10.
[36] *De Fide* 4.10.
[37] *De Fide* 4.10.
[38] *De Fide* 4.11.
[39] *De Fide* 4.11.

One will notice that John draws on highly sacramental and cov-
enantal language related to baptism and faith, noting in the broader
context that the sign of baptism relates to the sign of circumcision. While different modern denominations disagree about how
to articulate the relationship between the biblical covenants and the
sacraments/ordinances of the church, John nonetheless follows the
general biblical idiom of not-too-easily separating the acts of faith
and baptism. Most notably for our present purposes, John has a
whole-Bible view of God's salvation and its implications for believers. In *The Orthodox Faith*, he effortlessly moves from the triune
God, to his creation, to God becoming man, to mankind being
restored to God's created image-bearers. We see this culminate in
his teaching on the resurrection.

John ends *The Orthodox Faith* with a call to look forward to
eternity in the resurrection, "for there really will be . . . a resurrection of the dead."[40] The dignity and importance of mankind is
wrapped up in this resurrection hope, for animals have no such
hope and, indeed, "If there is no resurrection, there is no God and
no providence, and all things are being driven and carried along
by mere chance."[41] But since God has promised a resurrection
throughout Scripture, we should trust that "God is just and He
rewards those who await Him in patience."[42] Recall John's teaching
all the way back at the beginning of the third book: God's response
to sin is the long story of the Bible, where God teaches us our need
for salvation through both suffering and revelation, and ultimately
secures our redemption in the incarnation. If all of this is true, he

---

[40] *De Fide* 4.27.
[41] *De Fide* 4.27.
[42] *De Fide* 4.27.

reasons, then we can trust that God will continue to keep his promises. He concludes with an allusion to the eternal beatific vision for those who are raised with Christ:

> And those who have done good will shine like the sun together with the angels unto eternal life with our Lord Jesus Christ, ever seeing Him and being seen, enjoying the unending bliss which is from Him, and praising Him together with the Father and the Holy Ghost unto the endless ages of ages. Amen.[43]

Amen!

William Tyndale

Sixteenth-century English Reformer William Tyndale's legacy is largely wrapped up in his commitment to translating the Bible into English. Influenced by Luther and the Reformation—and, in particular, Luther's translation of the Bible into German—Tyndale sought to ensure that every believer could access Scripture in his or her own language. This was, of course, a reaction to the abuses of the late medieval Roman Catholic Church, which often only allowed clergymen to interpret Scripture for laypeople. For Tyndale, this was not merely an ecclesial authority issue, though it was; it was also, and perhaps primarily, a conviction that Christians could not know God truly if they could not themselves read Scripture under the illumination of the Holy Spirit. While the Reformers always had a deep desire to reform and renew the church, they did not want the ecclesial to eclipse or control the personal.

---

[43] *De Fide* 4.27.

As we saw previously in Luther, Tyndale viewed the OT and
NT as two "books." For example, he says this clearly in *A Pathway
into the Holy Scripture*:

> The Old Testament is a book, wherein is written the law
> of God, and the deeds of them which fulfil them, and of
> them also which fulfil them not. The New Testament is a
> book, wherein are contained the promises of God; and the
> deeds of them which believe them, or believe them not.[44]

For Tyndale, the gospel—which "signifieth good, merry, glad and
joyful tidings, that maketh a man's heart glad, and maketh him
sing, dance, and leap for joy"[45]—is found in both books. In the
OT, it is the promise of grace for those under the weight of the law;
in the NT, it is the fulfillment and proclamation of that promise by
Christ and the apostles.

So, when Tyndale considers how Scripture speaks to personal
and ecclesial communion with God, he does so with the premodern Christian sensibility that the biblical canon is a twofold or
unified witness to the gospel. In response to this twofold witness,
one's response to Scripture's explanation of the gospel determines
whether or not he understands the gospel. Tyndale offers several
characteristics of those who understand and those who do not.

On the one hand, there are two types of people who do not
understand the gospel and its relationship to the law. One group

---

[44] William Tyndale, *Doctrinal Treatises and Introductions to Different
Portions of the Holy Scriptures*, The Works of William Tyndale vol. 1, ed.
Henry Walter (Cambridge: Cambridge University, 1848), 8. All following
citations are from this work's edition of *A Pathway into the Holy Scripture*.
[45] Tyndale, *Doctrinal Treatises*, 8.

consists of those who do not understand the gospel, justify themselves by works, and condemn those who are not as outwardly righteous as they appear.[46] These are the self-righteous legalists who do not understand the need for grace. The other group consists of those who:

> give themselves unto all manner vices with full consent and full delectation, having no respect to the law of God . . . but say, God is merciful, and Christ died for us; supposing that such dreaming and imagination is that faith which is so greatly commended in holy scripture.[47]

These are a type of antinomian—those who believe that grace covers unabashed violations of God's law. For Tyndale, however, to disregard the law as obsolete, and thus sin without restraint, misunderstands the point of the law. Those who understand the gospel must also understand the goodness and usefulness of the law.

On the other hand, those who truly understand the gospel "have this right faith [and] consent to the law, that it is righteous and good."[48] Why is the law considered righteous and good? Because the law was meant to awaken sinners to their need for grace. In this way, the law functions positively as a way to help sinners understand God's character and to understand their desperate need for his grace. Those who have this right faith ultimately (1) know that God is the author of the law, knowing that the law must then be good; (2) desire to obey the law, knowing they cannot fully do so because of their sinful nature; and (3) hate the things

---

[46] Tyndale, 12.
[47] Tyndale, 12.
[48] Tyndale, 13.

that the law forbids, knowing that the law rightly condemns that which is sinful.[49]

Those who have this "right faith," then, look to Christ, the fulfiller of the gospel promises in the OT. The Christian's works are simply an outworking of the grace of the gospel. Tyndale offers three benefits of good works. "First, they certify us that we are heirs of everlasting life," who by the Holy Spirit have the power to (albeit imperfectly) obey the law. "And secondarily, we tame the flesh therewith," by walking in dependence on the Holy Spirit. "And thirdly, we do our duty unto our neighbour," reflecting the gospel and thereby drawing people to honor and praise God.[50]

Just like those before him, Tyndale saw right interpretation of Scripture as a holy act that fosters communion with God. Indeed, he argued that this view of the gospel in Scripture "is to have all the scripture unlocked and opened before thee; so that if thou wilt go in, and read, thou canst not but understand."[51] To understand Scripture as God's unified revelation in Christ is to understand "right faith" that works itself out in word and deed.

Conclusion

What would be the point of being taught by God if we were not willing to ask him the final question, how then should we live? "All Scripture," Paul says, "is inspired by God and is profitable for teaching, for rebuking, for correcting, for training in righteousness, so that the man of God may be complete, equipped for every good

---

[49] Tyndale, 13.
[50] Tyndale, 23.
[51] Tyndale, 23.

work" (2 Tim 3:16–17). This means that all Scripture is ultimately meant to transform us both personally and as Christ's body.

Martyr showed us that a theological-Christological sensibility leads ultimately to personal and ecclesial transformation, for Christianity is ultimately the true philosophy that makes sense of reality and patterns how we live within this reality. Augustine of Hippo's view on human frailty and the desperate need for God's radical, external grace led him emphasize that all interpretation should eventually lead to right living. John of Damascus reminds us that as we read Scripture, God is always pointing our eyes to the new creation, when God will bring an end to sin and death and usher in all of his promises for his people. Tyndale, though certainly a Reformer of the late medieval Roman Catholic Church, taught that the church should not be abandoned for some sort of lone-wolf Christianity, but rather that God desires that his church have access to the Word so they might be able to hear the address of God himself in the text.

Modern Christians often jump quickly to this "application." In many of the evangelical circles I have encountered, a three-point moral lesson is all the audience may receive from a sermon. But pre-modern interpreters give us a better balance—we can only "apply" Scripture to our own lives and churches by first understanding the way the words go and the unity found on God's providence, the Son's incarnation, and the Spirit's indwelling and illumination. Being taught by God requires diligent, Spirit-led interpretation that seeks to hear from God as he has revealed himself in Scripture.

5

Moving Forward by Looking Back: Three Reasons to Retrieve the Christian Tradition

We should not be afraid of the early church and their approach to Scripture.

During my early training as a pastor and theologian, many of my mentors warned me that emulating the interpretive methods of the early church is a dangerous game. The concerns were typically twofold. First, there was the concern that the patristic and medieval eras were forerunners to Roman Catholicism, and so their exegetical method and theological conclusions were inherently opposed to the tenets of the Protestant Reformation. Secondly, they were concerned that the so-called "allegorical" elements of the early church's approach, which are seen as dangerously unbound from the biblical text, enabled the interpreter to make Scripture say whatever he or she wants it to say. At worst, they said, the early church was guilty of "not doing exegesis" but rather "theologizing the text beyond the human author's intent."

The method that I was handed instead placed a high emphasis on attempting to re-create the historical background of the text and/or a painstaking psychoanalysis of the human author. To understand the Bible, some said, we have to put ourselves in the shoes of the Israelite and Greco-Roman people who first wrote and heard these stories and letters. I remember reading Benjamin Jowett's infamous essay on interpretation, in which he argued,

> Scripture has one meaning—the meaning which it had in
> the mind of the Prophet or Evangelist who first uttered or
> wrote, to the hearers or readers who first received it. . . .
> The true use of interpretation is to *get rid of* interpretation,
> and leave us alone in company with the author.[1]

Frankly, I found this approach to be not only against the grain of the Bible's claims about God's transforming word and witness (e.g., 2 Tim 3:16–17), but also impossible—there is no time machine waiting to take us back to these cultures, so all history is a type of reconstruction of known facts. Whatever interpretive help we may glean from attempting to understand the original context of the biblical writings—and this is a worthy goal!—we cannot stop there.

---

[1] Benjamin Jowett, "On the Interpretation of Scripture," *Essays and Reviews*, 7th ed. (London: Longman, Green, Longman, and Roberts, 1861), 378 and 384, emphasis mine.

The Bible is not a mere history book, but "living and effective" due to its everlasting divine source and subject matter (Heb 4:12).[2]

Thus, when I was introduced to the patristic writers in particular, my love for God and Scripture was revived in a way I could not have imagined. Their clear insistence on God as not only the source but also the subject matter or point of Scripture grabbed ahold of me. Contrary to the concerns of some of my mentors, they cared about both elements of the text—the human authorial intent and the divine Author's larger story. They showed me in practice what I was intuitively wrestling with: we cannot treat the Bible as just another piece of ancient literature, but rather God's special and unique word to his people, with a story centered on the saving work of Christ and the indwelling of the Holy Spirit. We have two thousand years of believers who have imperfectly but faithfully sought to know God by dwelling deeply on his Word. As Augustine argues, we should read Scripture ultimately to see the face of God,[3] and the early church can help us do that.

It is worth noting at this juncture that the concerns noted above can be legitimate. Certainly, most Protestants would disagree with many of the early church's theological and interpretive conclusions, especially with respect to ecclesiology (which, of course, is largely informed by exegesis). Further, we see in certain patristic and medieval writers an "allegorical" tendency that might seem wild to us or just plain speculative—though I have shown already the complications with maintaining a single definition of allegory in the early church. Any discerning reader can make judgments about

---

[2] Of course, Heb 4:12 has an underlying assumption that this "living and effective" Word is inextricably tied to Christ himself, the Son and Word who reveals the Father (Heb 1:1–2).

[3] *Exp. Ps.* 10.11.

the worthiness of any single interpreter's conclusions—ancient or modern—but our great cloud of historical witnesses call out to us, and we ought to lend them an ear.

What Is Retrieval and Why Should We Care?

Learning from and applying insights from the early church requires us to do retrieval. Simply put, retrieval is the act of reading and understanding those who have come before us as a way to apply encouragement and/or correction for renewal in today's church. Timothy George offered a valuable extended definition in a recent lecture:

> What is retrieval? It is not just refurbishment. It is not just going back and finding something or someone famous four or five hundred years ago and dusting them off and letting them shine again in all of their glory. There is nothing wrong with that, but more is involved in retrieval. Retrieval is more of a rescue operation—it recognizes that there is a great deal of our Christian past that has become obscure, that we just don't know about anymore. Retrieval looks at these figures as our fellow sojourners in the life of faith. We are one with them in Jesus Christ. They are guiding lights for the people of God throughout the ages. That sometimes means we have to ask new and different questions of them, different from what they were asking in their own day. We have the right, and even the responsibility, to do just that.[4]

---

[4] This is my transcription of a portion of George's 2017 Simon J. Kistemaker lecture at Reformed Theological Seminary in Orlando, FL. His lecture and the others from the Simon J. Kistemaker Academic

This type of retrieval—understanding the past and applying insights today—requires patience, diligence, wisdom, and moral virtue. Let me explain why.

In order to understand those who have come before us, we must first do responsible historical theology. The preceding chapters are an attempt to model responsible historical theology by faithfully and fairly representing past figures in their own context and idiom. Neither Athanasius nor Martin Luther are twenty-first-century Christians. While some of their concerns are similar to ours—namely, the continual pull toward heresies of various similar kinds—they were men of their time. Just as we would want someone in the future to represent our beliefs fairly and generously, we should do the same for those before us. This will take patience and diligence to read them closely and work through what we can take (or leave) from their works. Then, and only then, can we reflect on how these premodern interpreters might help us better read our Bibles today.

In order to apply the insights of those before us, we must use wisdom and be careful to practice moral virtue. It is tempting to retrieve the Christian tradition merely as a way to win a current theological war. If we are not careful, we can end up pillaging and weaponizing the past to divide the church and/or take down everyone and everything we dislike in today's church. This is why responsible historical theology is important; it restrains our tendency to fashion past figures into heroes of our own making. Here is a good test that I try to (imperfectly) apply to myself when doing historical theology and retrieval: Am I reading a past figure or topic

---

Lecture Series can be accessed online at https://rts.edu/campuses/orlando/community/kistemaker-lectures/.

because someone has angered me or needs a good theo-slap, or am I doing it to build up the saints and advance the gospel with treasures of old? There are times when retrieval serves a good and necessary purpose for fighting heresy in our day. Yes, and amen! But our default posture should be to retrieve the past as a way to highlight the beauty of two-millennia of Christian thought as a better way forward for the church, not as a way to fight miniature modern battles the way the world would have us fight them. Fighting with the world's weapons of scorn and slander ultimately diminishes the beauty of Christian belief rather than highlighting it.

To conclude, below are three reasons to retrieve the interpretive approach of our Christian forebears. I hope this will encourage readers to care more about retrieval for the renewal of our church today. In short, I pray that by looking back at the saints who have come before us, we can move forward as saints seeking to be faithful to Scripture in our own day.

1. To Learn in Humility

You are not the first person to ever read the Bible. Neither am I! Reading other interpreters is a way to practice humility, recognizing that we need help in understanding Scripture. I often tell my students, most of whom are in their late teens or early twenties, that they should view their growth in Christian knowledge and wisdom as a marathon, not a sprint. Reading Scripture well requires re-reading Scripture again and again. We will never fully understand and grasp all of Scripture. We will never have a perfect, inerrant interpretation. We need help.

Scripture often calls us to remember those who have come before us. In both the OT and NT, remembrance is a way for God's people to humble themselves before the Lord who has been at work before them and will continue to be at work after. Israel was often pointed back to the exodus event as a way to remember God's power and faithful love for generations after the event (Lev 26:13; Num 15:41; Deut 6:12; Ps 95:7–11). Later NT authors would also use memory as a way to humble their audience by telling them to trust the Lord unlike the Israelites in the wilderness (1 Cor 10:1–13; Heb 3:7–19) or to let the testimonies of the saints before spur us on (Hebrews 11). In a similar way, we can remember the saints whom God has continued to use throughout church history, humbling ourselves by remembering God's good work in them, and gleaning what we can—both good and bad—to be faithful in our own generation to how God is speaking through his Word.

2. To Anchor Ourselves

In every generation, the world around us can seem hopeless. Death, taxes, and the sinfulness of mankind are sure things. If you feel the ocean is unsettled and even violent, anchor yourself to the saints who have come before. As C. S. Lewis famously argued in a preface to Athanasius's *On the Incarnation*, "Every age has its own outlook. It is specially good at seeing certain truths and specially liable to make certain mistakes. We all, therefore, need the books that will correct the characteristic mistakes of our own period. And that means the old books."[5] Put another way, those who have come before think and speak differently than us. This is not to say that

---

[5] C. S. Lewis, "Preface," in Athanasius of Alexandria, *On the Incarnation*, trans. John Behr (Yonkers, NY: SVS, 2011), 10.

the past is more correct than we are today, but rather that a different idiom and set of assumptions can challenge our way of thinking. When we read premodern interpreters, we are reading people in often completely different contexts and situations. Many of them are not motivated to answer challenges set forth by the scientific revolution or the advancement of artificial intelligence. These are questions for our own day that must be taken seriously, but these questions can sometimes consume us such that we miss the bigger picture of God's work in the world throughout history. Reading those who have come before us can anchor us to the Word of God that has endured through the ages and has been relevant in every one of them.

3. To Worship with the Church

I was tempted to add a fourth sensibility to this book—reading Scripture with the church. For much of Christian history, part of understanding Scripture was understanding Scripture through the eyes of faithful Christians who had come before. Certainly, this impulse could cause the reader to rely on secondary sources rather than reading Scripture itself, but this does not have to be the case. The real upshot of reading those who have come before is to worship with God's people throughout space and time. Since humanity was first formed from the dust and given life by the breath of God, every human who has breathed and then returned to the dust has been an image-bearer of God.

And those who faithfully worship their Creator have been called his covenant people and, even if dead, are more intimately related to us today than our closest relatives. When we abandon the past and keep our eyes only on the present, we ignore the family

God has been building for millennia. Like teenagers who shun the wisdom of their elders, we can tend to slam the doors to our generation's bedroom and convince ourselves that the only meaningful truth lies within our bedroom walls. But as mature adults one day recognize, our elders had much wisdom to pass along. Indeed, we often say, "I sound like my father!" or "I finally understand what my mother meant when she said that." This type of maturity is required in God's family of interpreters who are taught by God, as we all seek to grow in wisdom and worship together in truth, from generation to generation, as sojourners together to the New Jerusalem. Matthew Emerson and Luke Stamps say it well: "As we retrieve the past, we seek to renew the present and to ready ourselves for the future, when all of God's people will at last be one even as our great triune God is one (Jn 17:11)."[6]

---

[6] Matthew Y. Emerson and R. Lucas Stamps, "Conclusion: Toward an Evangelical Baptist Catholicity," in *Baptists and the Christian Tradition: Towards an Evangelical Baptist Catholicity*, ed. Matthew Y. Emerson, Christopher W. Morgan, and R. Lucas Stamps (Nashville: B&H Academic, 2020), 355.

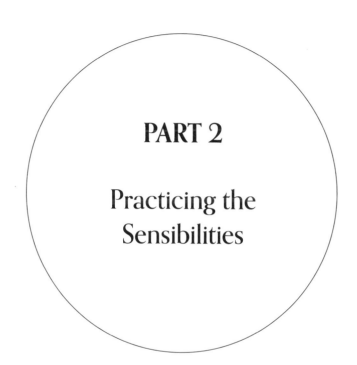

PART 2

Practicing the Sensibilities

6

The Judgment of Death and the Staff of Life: Numbers 16-17

S cripture is meant to be proclaimed by God's people.

Thus far, we have considered three sensibilities that have historically characterized premodern interpretation. First, we explored the letter and history—the way the words go. Throughout the Christian tradition, the text itself and the history it presents have been largely assumed. There is no "meaning" to be found apart from the words and stories of Scripture. Next, we looked at the theological and Christological unity of Scripture—how it fits together. The Christian tradition has always assumed that there is a unity to God's revelation in Scripture, because God is the primary author and subject, and God is not and cannot be confused. Of course, the key to understanding how the Bible fits together is the Son who took on flesh and dwelt among us—the one of whom the OT spoke, and the one of whom the NT continued to speak. Finally, we considered how Scripture impacts personal and ecclesial communion with God—how to live in light of its truths. It has been a common assumption for all of Christian history that Scripture does not terminate on mere words or ideas, but that the Spirit works to transform its readers.

In the following chapters, I will present four examples of applying these sensibilities to the biblical text—two from OT texts and two from NT texts. My hope here is simply to provide *one way* Christians can read the biblical text along the same path as the great cloud of witnesses who have come before us. For each text, I will provide a brief introduction on the sensibilities' function in the passage, followed by an application of these sensibilities in what amounts to an exegetical essay or sermon manuscript.

Numbers 16-17

In this text, the sensibilities are worked out in various ways. In terms of letter and history, we can note the context of Numbers 16–17 in light of its book-level context and larger OT context. Who are the main characters and why are they important to the story? Moses is obviously the Israelites' prophet who leads them through the wilderness. Korah and some of his friends have shown up elsewhere in Scripture, and that helps frame their interaction with Moses. Further, an important aspect of letter and history is following "the way the words go," so we let the flow of the text inform our interpretation.

In terms of a theological-Christological thread, we consider who God is in this passage. How is God presented in Scripture?

What must be true of him and his interactions with his people in the text? Not only that, but we cannot ignore that this text does not terminate on the original readers or "intended audience," but has something to contribute to the biblical story. Noting the themes, motifs, or ideas that are present in this text forms a foundation for considering how they appear elsewhere in Scripture and in light of Christ. The story of Moses and the Israelites is, ultimately, a piece of a larger biblical narrative.

Finally, this text has something to say to us today. The danger here is jumping to an application too quickly. This can lead to strained moral principles that do not reflect the point of the text or its fulfillment in Christ and the Holy Spirit. But by following the way the words go and considering the unity of God and his revelation in Christ, we can draw out personal or ecclesial "applications" that are faithful to the text.

Introduction

Throughout the book of Numbers, the Israelites rebel against Moses's leadership and ultimately against God's plan for them. They complain about not having enough food to eat, about being tired of wandering in the wilderness, and about the enemies they run across along the way. And every time, even at his worst, Moses ultimately reminds them of God's faithfulness and at times even begs God to forgive them.

Some scholars have estimated that there were anywhere from a few hundred thousand to as many as two million Israelites in the wilderness with Moses. Can you imagine a population the size of the Greater Nashville area looking at you, grumbling and complaining and whining about their circumstances? This really puts Moses's situation into perspective. He is trying to follow God's call to lead this massive group of people, and oftentimes the only thanks he gets is more complaining. And then we come to Numbers 16–17, where the community's rebellion against Moses turns up a notch.

Rebellion against God and His Appointed Leaders

The story begins with rebellion in Num 16:1–13:

> Now Korah son of Izhar, son of Kohath, son of Levi, with Dathan and Abiram, sons of Eliab, and On son of Peleth, sons of Reuben, took two hundred and fifty prominent Israelite men who were leaders of the community and representatives in the assembly, and they rebelled against Moses. They came together against Moses and Aaron and told them, "You have gone too far! Everyone in the entire community is holy, and the LORD is among them. Why then do you exalt yourselves above the LORD's assembly?"
>
> When Moses heard this, he fell facedown. Then he said to Korah and all his followers, "Tomorrow morning the LORD will reveal who belongs to him, who is set apart, and the one he will let come near him. He will let the one he chooses come near him. Korah, you and all your followers are to do this: take firepans, and tomorrow place fire in them and put incense on them before the LORD. Then the man the LORD chooses will be the one who is set apart. It is you Levites who have gone too far!"
>
> Moses also told Korah, "Now listen, Levites! Isn't it enough for you that the God of Israel has separated you from the Israelite community to bring you near to himself,

to perform the work at the LORD's tabernacle, and to stand before the community to minister to them? He has brought you near, and all your fellow Levites who are with you, but you are pursuing the priesthood as well. Therefore, it is you and all your followers who have conspired against the Lord! As for Aaron, who is he that you should complain about him?"

Moses sent for Dathan and Abiram, the sons of Eliab, but they said, "We will not come! Is it not enough that you brought us up from a land flowing with milk and honey to kill us in the wilderness? Do you also have to appoint yourself as ruler over us?"

There are a couple of things to notice right away. First, in verses 1–2, we see four men leading this rebellion of 250 Israelite leaders. Korah is Moses's and Aaron's cousin, and he's Kohath's son, which means his family lineage was appointed by God in Numbers 4 to help transport the furnishings of the tabernacle. This was one of the highest callings in the land. Korah, as the leader of this clan, is therefore in one of the most prominent positions in the community.

Then, there's Dathan, Abiram, and On. The text says that they're "sons of Reuben." The last time we saw Reuben, back in Genesis 49, he had forfeited his birthright to leadership in the community because he slept with his father's girlfriend. So, we have Korah, who has one of the highest positions in the community wanting even more power, and we have the three Reubenites who seemingly want power because their ancestors forfeited the power they think they should have.

Notice their claim against Moses and Aaron: "They came together against Moses and Aaron and told them, 'You have gone too far! Everyone in the entire community is holy, and the LORD is among them. Why then do you exalt yourselves above the LORD's assembly?'" Then, in verse 3, they falsely accuse Moses and Aaron of exalting themselves above them. This is an important claim, since the biblical story shows that Moses was commissioned by God to lead the Israelites. Consider his initial interaction with God in Exod 3:9–11 and Exod 4:10–13:

> "So because the Israelites' cry for help has come to me, and I have also seen the way the Egyptians are oppressing them, therefore, go. I am sending you to Pharaoh so that you may lead my people, the Israelites, out of Egypt." But Moses asked God, "Who am I that I should go to Pharaoh and that I should bring the Israelites out of Egypt?" . . .
>
> But Moses replied to the LORD, "Please, Lord, I have never been eloquent—either in the past or recently or since you have been speaking to your servant—because my mouth and my tongue are sluggish." The LORD said to him, "Who placed a mouth on humans? Who makes a person mute or deaf, seeing or blind? Is it not I, the LORD? Now go! I will help you speak and I will teach you what to say."
>
> Moses said, "Please, Lord, send someone else."

According to the larger OT context, Moses has often been extremely passive and uncomfortable with leading Israel. And yet these men, one of whom is his own cousin, are accusing him of exalting himself. Korah and the others say "the entire community is holy" as a reason for why Moses shouldn't be in charge. Perhaps they think everyone should be equal; yet God put Moses in the position of leadership. So, it seems, they have become bitter against both Moses and God.

Now, in this moment, Moses has two options for responding to these accusations: (1) he can start a civil war; (2) he can immediately turn to the Lord and not retaliate. He chooses option 2: "When Moses heard this, he fell facedown" (Num 16:4). He immediately humbles himself, falls facedown, and gives the situation to the Lord. Moses knows that he's done nothing wrong. He knows he does not deserve this kind of treatment. But instead of sticking out his chest, he puts his face on the ground.

Then, Moses tries to reason with them:

> He has brought you near, and all your fellow Levites who are with you, but you are pursuing the priesthood as well. Therefore, it is you and all your followers who have conspired against the LORD! As for Aaron, who is he that you should complain about him? (vv. 10–11)

Moses basically says, "You have been raised up and appointed by God to do great things, but now you want more. It's not me you have a problem with, but God. He's the one who has placed us in our roles in the community." Dathan and Abiram's response would be funny if it weren't so sad: "Moses sent for Dathan and Abiram, the sons of Eliab, but they said, 'We will not come! Is it not enough that you brought us up from a land flowing with milk and honey to kill us in the wilderness? Do you also have to appoint yourself as ruler over us?'" (vv. 12–13).

They say, "You brought us from a land flowing with milk and honey." What land are they talking about here? Egypt, the place of slavery. Again, they idolize their slavery in Egypt as being better than being free and in the wilderness with God. God promised to give them the Promised Land, a land flowing with milk and honey, but they are so twisted at this point that they're calling Egypt the Promised Land.

So, as the story goes, Moses suggests that they all present incense before the Lord. This was a priestly action of burning up incense, and the idea is that the smell of the burning incense would rise up to the Lord and he would accept or reject the offering based on the aroma. God's answer to whose offering he accepted is clear in verse 20: "The LORD spoke to Moses and Aaron, 'Separate yourselves from this community so I may consume them instantly.'"

Moses's Forgiveness and Sacrifice

Now, we have already seen at this point that this group is trying to overthrow God's plan and doubting his goodness in placing Moses and Aaron in leadership, and in bringing them into the wilderness. So, it is no surprise that God rejects their offering—and then says he is going to destroy everyone, not just the ones who rebelled this time. But Moses again pleads with God:

> But Moses and Aaron fell facedown and said, "God, God who gives breath to all, when one man sins, will you vent your wrath on the whole community?" The LORD replied to Moses, "Tell the community: Get away from the dwellings of Korah, Dathan, and Abiram." Moses got up and went to Dathan and Abiram, and the elders of Israel followed him. He warned the community, "Get away now from the tents of these wicked men. Don't touch anything that belongs to them, or you will be swept away because of all their sins." (Num 16:22–26)

Moses appeals to God's character as the God of life. Now, on the one hand, God could destroy everyone and be totally justified. The book of Numbers shows that, at various times, the entire community has turned their back on God, grumbled against him, and rebelled against Moses. These people are not innocent. One could argue that Moses would be justified in asking for their punishment. But even though they might have deserved punishment, Moses again falls facedown before God and begs him to spare them. Moses models radical forgiveness to those who have rebelled against him.

This pleading by Moses required sacrifice. God told him to step aside so that destruction would fall upon everyone, but he stood in front of God and shielded them, asking God to spare them. Not only that, but he sacrifices his own comfort, because the Lord knows these people are going to grumble again and make his life miserable again.

As an aside, why does God listen to Moses? God is sovereign and all-knowing and perfect. He could destroy everyone and be justified in doing so as the perfect judge. Did God change his mind? Was God confused? These questions seem like the wrong ones to focus on here. What we should notice is that God heard Moses's prayer and honored his request. God answers prayer. Moses's radical, humble, loving, sacrificial prayer had an actual impact on the world. God is sovereign and perfect and wholly beyond us, and yet at the same time he is extremely near to us, ready to listen to our prayers and even grant our requests.

Back to Moses, let us further consider his sacrificial act here. Consider Num 16:41–48:

> The next day the entire Israelite community complained about Moses and Aaron, saying, "You have killed the Lord's people!" When the community assembled against them, Moses and Aaron turned toward the tent of meeting,

and suddenly the cloud covered it, and the LORD's glory appeared. Moses and Aaron went to the front of the tent of meeting, and the LORD said to Moses, "Get away from this community so that I may consume them instantly." But they fell facedown. Then Moses told Aaron, "Take your firepan, place fire from the altar in it, and add incense. Go quickly to the community and make atonement for them, because wrath has come from the LORD; the plague has begun." He stood between the dead and the living, and the plague was halted.

Although Moses begged God to spare them from judgment, they overlook his forgiveness and sacrifice for them and immediately start complaining about him. They have already seen God destroy Korah and those who rebelled with him, and yet their hearts have not softened. Though it must be arduous to lead such a grumbling people, Moses again and again offers forgiveness and sacrifices his own comfort for them.

God's Response

In Num 17:1–8, God responds:

The LORD instructed Moses: "Speak to the Israelites and take one staff from them for each ancestral tribe, twelve staffs from all the leaders of their tribes. Write each man's name on his staff. Write Aaron's name on Levi's staff, because there is to be one staff for the head of each tribe. Then place them in the tent of meeting in front of the testimony where I meet with you. The staff of the man I choose will sprout, and I will rid myself of the Israelites' complaints that they have been making about you."

So Moses spoke to the Israelites, and each of their leaders gave him a staff, one for each of the leaders of their tribes, twelve staffs in all. Aaron's staff was among them. Moses placed the staffs before the Lord in the tent of the testimony. The next day Moses entered the tent of the testimony and saw that Aaron's staff, representing the house of Levi, had sprouted, formed buds, blossomed, and produced almonds!

Korah and the others tried to take Moses and Aaron's place as leaders of the community. Aaron in particular was the highest-ranking priest in the community. He was the one charged with offering sacrifices for the people's sins. God had appointed Aaron to this role, but reiterates it here for everyone to see. Aaron's staff looks like an ordinary staff lying there next to everyone else's, but his is the only one that sprouts almonds, a sign of life.

When Aaron's staff sprouts almonds, it means that God ordained Aaron to be the chief priest who made atonement for the people, covering their sins and giving them life. God reiterates here what he had already put into place—that one man would be responsible for atoning for the sins of the people. So, how does this fit into the larger storyline, and what does it mean for us?

The Comfort and Challenge of Christ

Scripture is God's self-revelation. We know the words of Paul, that "all Scripture is inspired by God and is profitable for teaching, for rebuking, for correcting, for training in righteousness, so that the man of God may be complete, equipped for every good work" (2 Tim 3:16–17). This Book that we read and seek to interpret is God's Word. It is in those pages that we hear from God and are transformed by his Spirit.

Further, a cursory reading of Scripture shows us that Scripture is a unified witness, if nothing else because Scripture itself is so self-referential. One notices rather easily that the NT regularly quotes or alludes to the OT and recapitulates its various themes and types (e.g., kingship, priesthood, sacrifice, et al.). Not only that, but the OT quotes and alludes to other OT books (e.g., the continual referring back to creation or the exodus event), and the NT has its own self-reference (e.g., Peter claiming that Paul's letters are Scripture in 2 Pet 3:16). Jesus says clearly on many occasions that the OT spoke about him and he refers to the OT to back up claims about himself, a practice that the NT authors will continue (Luke 24:27; John 5:39; Rom 15:4; 2 Pet 1:21; Heb 1:1–2).

How to View Numbers 16-17 in Light of the Gospel

Thus far, we have seen the character and providence of God as his people rebel against his plans. We saw Moses and Aaron staying true to God and his calling—leading the people and sacrificing for them even at their worst. In many ways, Moses and Aaron pass a test—the people deserve judgment, and yet they forgive their kinsmen and stand in their place before God. And while the theological-Christological connections are not as "obvious" as in other passages, Christians on this side of the cross and empty tomb should still ask how we might read this account in light of Christ.

Numbers 16–17 is Christian Scripture. Here are three ways we can reflect on this passage in light of the gospel.

1. We are invited to worship the true God.

Cyprian of Carthage pointed out the clear distinction between true vs. false worship in this passage in relationship to our own worship:

> The argument that [heretics] acknowledge the same God the Father, the same son Christ and the same Holy Spirit is no use to them either. Korah, Dathan and Abiram acknowledged the same God as Aaron the priest and Moses. They lived by the same law and the same religious practices, invoking the one true God who should properly be worshiped and invoked. All the same, when they went beyond the limits of their own ministry and claimed for themselves authority to perform sacrifices in opposition to Aaron the priest, who had received the lawful priesthood by the favor of God and the ordination of the Lord, they were struck from on high and at once paid the penalty for their unlawful attempt. The sacrifices which they offered impiously and unlawfully against God's will and ordinance could be neither valid nor efficacious.[1]

When we read this passage, we read it in light of God's providence and revelation in the Son and Holy Spirit. We may be among God's

---

[1] Cyprian of Carthage, *Letter* 69.8. Translation from *Exodus, Leviticus, Numbers, Deuteronomy*, ed. Joseph T. Lienhard and Ronnie J. Rombs, Ancient Christian Commentary on Scripture (Downers Grove, IL: InterVarsity, 2001), 229.

people in a local church and fellowship. We may read the Bible and sing the songs. But we should be warned to obey God's claims and commands in Scripture and not allow our own pride to create an idol in place of God, or even claim to worship the true God while seeking our own gain.

2. We are challenged to see ourselves as rebels.

When we look at Moses, we might be tempted to think that if that is what forgiveness looks like, we cannot live up. I am not sure I would have been so patient and kind. But most of us are not Moses. The truth is, we are often a lot more like Korah. We can be vindictive, vengeful, short-tempered, selfish, and unforgiving. We like to think we can be Moses or we are Moses, but that is not the point of the story.

Of course, Moses was not perfect by any stretch. He was a godly man, no doubt, but he had his flaws. But when we read this story with ourselves in the place of Korah and the other rebels, we see a fuller picture of ourselves. If they had been sacrificially forgiving, they would've trusted in God's sovereignty even in their anger and frustration about their circumstances. Their greatest sin was being bitter—unforgiving—toward God and Moses. They were bitter about their situation and about the wrong they felt had been done to them. They did not trust God's good plan, and so they did not obey God.

We are challenged here to realize that we are much more like Korah than Moses. We are often unwilling to forgive God and others for our situation. We pursue radical autonomy. But understanding this gives us a good picture of the state of our hearts and our need for God's mercy.

3. *We are comforted by God's forgiveness through Christ.*

So if we are Korah in this story, then who is Moses? Moses is a picture of Christ.

Christ is the one who continually forgives those who rebel against him. Christ is the one who did nothing wrong, and yet was still mocked and ridiculed and accused by his people. Christ is the one who stood in our place, between death and life, taking on the triune God's wrath toward sin in our place. When God said, "I should punish them for their rebellion," Christ fell facedown on the cross, making atonement for our sins. True sacrificial forgiveness.

And this time it was not Aaron's ordinary staff that sprang up with life so that people's sins could be forgiven. No, it was Christ's own bloodied, broken body. What looked like an ordinary man lying dead in any ordinary tomb turned out to be the sacrificial forgiveness needed to forgive all of us rebels. His resurrection means that once and for all, death is dead and sin is wiped clean. Forgiveness in its highest form.

We do not look to Aaron as a perpetual priest, offering sacrifices on our behalf. He served this purpose for a time, but he died and others took his place. Instead, he points us to Christ. Hebrews 7:26–28 says it this way:

> For this is the kind of high priest we need: holy, innocent, undefiled, separated from sinners, and exalted above the heavens. He doesn't need to offer sacrifices every day, as high priests do—first for their own sins, then for those of the people. He did this once for all time when he offered himself. For the law appoints as high priests men who are weak, but the promise of the oath, which came after the law, appoints a Son, who has been perfected forever.

Moses and Aaron were appointed by God to lead the people, but they were still sinners themselves. But Christ never sinned. This is the promise we rest on. A perfect priest. A perfect sacrifice. A priest who lives to intercede for us rebels. Jesus stands in heaven right now, eternally our high priest. Indeed, a priest and king that far exceeds Aaron and the Israelite priesthood (Heb 7:11–17).

4. We are invited to forgive.

Of course, this does not excuse us from being sacrificially forgiving, from pursuing the way of Moses and ultimately the way of Christ. We are often called to imitate Christ. God doesn't say, "Thanks to Jesus, you are all forgiven and free to continue to be little unforgiving Korahs." In fact, Jesus has strong words for us: "For if you forgive others their offenses, your heavenly Father will forgive you as well. But if you don't forgive others, your Father will not forgive your offenses" (Matt 6:14–15).

When we trust in Christ, we are sealed with the Holy Spirit (Eph 1:3–14). We have God living inside of us, empowering us to live new lives shaped not by our rebellion but by Christ's righteousness. See, for example, Eph 4:30–32:

> And don't grieve God's Holy Spirit. You were sealed by him for the day of redemption. Let all bitterness, anger and wrath, shouting and slander be removed from you, along with all malice. And be kind and compassionate to one another, forgiving one another, just as God also forgave you in Christ.

In other words, Christians cannot say that it is impossible to forgive. We can choose not to forgive, but it is no longer impossible. We are called to forgive others like the Father forgave us through Christ, and we are given the Holy Spirit in order to live out that forgiveness.

If we want to be Moses in this story, to know what sacrificial, forgiving love looks like, we need to look at the true and better Moses—Jesus Christ. On the cross we see both the forgiveness we need and the power we need to forgive others in the same way. Our Savior was abused and rejected and abandoned by the very people he came to save. Indeed, we are all Korah. The good news is that we do not have to forgive others in our own strength—we have the Holy Spirit to empower us to take steps toward reconciliation.

God's people are called to be a forgiving people. Forgiveness requires sacrifice. We cannot forgive others without first sacrificing our own pride to submit our lives to Christ, and we cannot forgive others without submitting to the Holy Spirit's power to help us. We have to fall facedown before God. This does not mean we forget about past sins. It does not mean we pretend like we have not been hurt. It means that in our hurt and in our anger and in our frustration, we can acknowledge sin while at the same time forgiving others the way we have been forgiven.

We can be like Korah and millions of others who choose to wage war, instead of striving for peace. Or we can look to Christ, whose sacrificial love brought us the forgiveness we did not deserve, so that we can offer forgiveness to those who do not deserve it. Christ, the true and better Moses, gives us the ability to be like Moses here, but only if his forgiveness changes us first.

7

A New Priesthood and Covenant to Come: Malachi 1-2

Moving to a different genre and portion of the OT, the sensibilities play out similarly in Malachi 1–2 as they did in Numbers 16–17. First, we are continually reminded to be sensitive to the way the words go. What is being claimed in the text? Who are the main characters and what are the main themes? In terms of theological-Christological unity, the book of Malachi sits at the end of the Book of the Twelve and the whole OT in the Christian canon. Its place in the canon urges the reader to reflect on all that has come before and look forward to what is ahead as the pages of the NT lie in wait. Finally, there are clear implications for personal and ecclesial life in Israel's struggles and failures to be obedient to the Lord.

Introduction

Whether Malachi is truly the last prophet of Israel or whether Malachi was written last among the Hebrew Scriptures is a debate easily found in biblical commentaries. This question is not unimportant, but threatens to distract us from the larger question: What has happened to Israel and its priests and what does this mean for Israel's past and future? And since it's placed at the end of the OT texts in the Christian canon, we are pressured to anticipate a resolution that doesn't come in Malachi, but will hopefully come in the following pages of the NT. We can start sorting out issues in Malachi 1–2 by looking at (1) the main details of the text and (2) the book's larger "disputation" structure.

First, there are several main details in the text that the biblical reader will notice. In particular, familiar characters and ideas from the OT form much of the narrative, particularly God calling Israel to account through a prophet and God's priests who are in charge of mediating between God and Israel. These details help us understand what's at stake: the Lord's judgment on his people and the question of how they can be forgiven.

Second, the book is structured around six "disputations"—a type of conversation between the Lord and his people. Our passages cover the first three disputations. The first disputation is Mal 1:2–5, where the Lord addresses his love for his people. The second disputation, making up nearly half of the entire book, is Mal 1:6–2:9, in which the Lord addresses the failure of the priests. The third disputation, in Mal 2:10–16, deals with God's "marriage" covenant to his people. Third, these disputations draw out the various ways Israel is in deep need of repentance and yet still part of the Lord's covenant promises. These three disputations ultimately set up the next three disputations, which return to these themes and both warn of forth-coming judgment and promise deliverance for Israel.

We will discuss each disputation in turn as three ways to see God's promise of deliverance coming to a head in anticipation for the coming Messiah and a new priesthood for God's people in desperate need of a mediator and an eternal hope of salvation.[1]

The First Disputation: God's Love for His People

God spoke to Israel through the prophet Malachi, reminding them, "'I have loved you,' says the LORD. Yet you ask, 'How have you loved us?'" (Mal 1:2a). Israel has turned away from God and are ignorant—or pretending to be ignorant—of how he has loved them throughout their history. Perhaps this concern is understandable, given that Israel had just returned from exile and are wondering anew what the Lord has for them. God responds by reminding them of Genesis 25:

> "Wasn't Esau Jacob's brother?" This is the LORD's declaration. "Even so, I loved Jacob, but I hated Esau. I turned his mountains into a wasteland, and gave his inheritance to the desert jackals." Though Edom says, "We have been devastated, but we will rebuild the ruins," the LORD of Armies says this: "They may build, but I will demolish. They will be called a wicked country and the people the LORD has cursed forever. Your own eyes will see this, and

---

[1] I am grateful to my colleagues Randall McKinion and Michael Shepherd for their contribution to my thinking on these passages.

you yourselves will say, 'The LORD is great, even beyond the borders of Israel.'" (Mal 1:2b–5)

In short, God reminds them of his election of Jacob to show that he has kept his promises to Israel and will, by his own decree and sovereign purpose, continue to preserve his people. Their unfaithfulness doesn't ultimately determine the Lord's faithfulness.

The Second Disputation: God's Concern about Failed Mediators

Again, this second disputation makes up about half of the book and describes in detail a major issue facing Israel: the old covenant has been broken, the priests are failed mediators, and God intends to deal with it. God starts by mentioning their complete disrespect for him:

> "A son honors his father, and a servant his master. But if I am a father, where is my honor? And if I am a master, where is your fear of me? says the LORD of Armies to you priests, who despise my name." Yet you ask, "How have we despised your name?" (Mal 1:6)

"Where is your fear of me?" is a piercing question, since the fear of the Lord is such an integral part of Israel's relationship to him. It's not merely that they should fear the Lord in terms of being afraid of his majesty and power (though this is part of it); rather, "The fear of the LORD is the beginning of wisdom, and the knowledge of the Holy One is understanding" (Prov 9:10). Fear of the Lord is related to wise obedience, a way of life that is centered on choosing God's commands over any other option the world could offer (Proverbs 1–2).

Israel has clearly been disobedient—they have not feared the Lord and turned to wisdom. Instead, they have defiled the Lord's table:

> "When you present a blind animal for sacrifice, is it not wrong? And when you present a lame or sick animal, is it not wrong? Bring it to your governor! Would he be pleased with you or show you favor?" asks the LORD of Armies. "And now plead for God's favor. Will he be gracious to us? Since this has come from your hands, will he show any of you favor?" asks the LORD of Armies. "I wish one of you would shut the temple doors, so that you would no longer kindle a useless fire on my altar! I am not pleased with you," says the LORD of Armies, "and I will accept no offering from your hands." (Mal 1:8–10)

Though all nations will ultimately bow to the Lord, he reminds them, his own people "scorn" having to worship him (Mal 1:11–13). It's gotten so bad that the Lord tells the people to shut the temple doors. Again, "the covenant of Levi" is a thing of the past. The people have broken it and there appears to be no plan to return to it. Instead, the Lord himself will keep the covenant.

The Lord reminds them that,

> "My covenant with [Levi] was one of life and peace, and I gave these to him; it called for reverence, and he revered me and stood in awe of my name. True instruction was in his mouth, and nothing wrong was found on his lips. He walked with me in peace and integrity and turned many from iniquity. For the lips of a priest should guard knowledge, and people should desire instruction from his mouth, because he is the messenger of the LORD of Armies." (Mal 2:5–7)

In Num 6:13–27, God lays out acceptable sacrifices, which
included unblemished animals and a mediator ("a Nazrite") who
would consecrate himself to the Lord and offer the sacrifice with
the appropriate reverence. The Lord's face would shine upon this
person as one who is blessed and acceptable to God. Further,
in Deut 33:8–11, the Lord gave specific instructions for priests
to teach rightly and bring acceptable offerings for the people.
Instead, the priests in Malachi's day offer blind animals with
unrepentant hearts, and thus the Lord's face is no longer shin-
ing on them. The Levites even rallied together against those who
worshipped the golden calf (Exod 32:25–29). These postexilic
priests in Malachi's day had clearly fallen far below expectations.
But, again, the Lord's faithfulness isn't determined by the people's
unfaithfulness.

The Third Disputation: God's Call for Covenant Faithfulness

The third disputation begins with a question and rebuke, this time
from Malachi to the people:

> Don't all of us have one Father? Didn't one God create
> us? Why then do we act treacherously against one another,
> profaning the covenant of our ancestors? Judah has acted
> treacherously, and a detestable act has been done in Israel
> and in Jerusalem. For Judah has profaned the LORD's sanc-
> tuary, which he loves, and has married the daughter of a
> foreign god. (Mal 2:10–11)

The language here is in some sense a continuation of the previous
disputation. Just as God reminds them that he is their Father, so

Malachi reminds them that beyond all ancestral fathers of Israel is God, the Father and Creator of all.

Further, I think the marriage example here is primarily a metaphor about God's covenant with his people. Israel is the husband and the wife is the covenant. Just as the priests have defiled the Lord's table and brought disdain upon the people and the temple, so Malachi rebukes them for idolatry ("marrying the daughter of a foreign god"). One could say that this disputation is speaking more "literally" about actual marriage and divorce among the Israelite people, and this interpretation is certainly possible. It would still show that the Israelites have fallen into serious sinful practices. However, it seems more likely that this is a metaphor about their covenant with God, given that false/failed worship and idolatry are at the heart of these disputations. Indeed, the final three disputations continue to focus on God's covenant with his people and their issues related to covenant-breaking.

The wisdom and fear of God make an appearance once again: "Even though the LORD has been a witness between you and the wife of your youth, you have acted treacherously against her. She was your marriage partner and your wife by covenant" (Mal 2:14; Prov 2:17). The Israelites are thus warned to be faithful to their covenant to the Lord by way of this analogy of the wise husband who is faithful to his wife. Similar to the story of Hosea and Gomer, God is faithful to his "marriage" covenant even when his wife is not.

Looking Ahead at God's Faithfulness

It's important to remember that underneath these disputations is the promise that God is a covenant-keeping God who intends to rescue his people. As you turn the page from the end of Malachi to the opening of Matthew's Gospel, you are reminded that God is "with" his people in the birth of their Messiah, Jesus Christ—the eternal Son who put on flesh and dwelt among us (Matt 1:23; John 1:14). The failure of Israel, the call for temple-closure, the promise of judgment were all real rebukes, but they were not the end. The covenant-keeping God would make all things new—and he would step into the world and save it from the inside out. God the Son would relive Israel's story, keep the covenant, and redeem his people.

When one reads the Gospels, it's clear that Israel is still in the same shape as when Malachi left them. They should have closed the temple doors and repented, but they obviously didn't. Instead, the temple had become a marketplace rather than a place of worship; sacrifices were being bought and sold; and the priests were against their own Messiah (e.g., Luke 5:14; John 2:16; Acts 21:26). And when they were rebuked by the Lord standing in front of them, the scenes from Malachi are brought back to mind.

For example, in John 8:12–20, Jesus offers for the Lord's face to shine on disobedient Israel once again: "Jesus spoke to them again: 'I am the light of the world. Anyone who follows me will never walk in the darkness but will have the light of life'" (John 8:12). When the Pharisees rebuke him for claiming to have divine authority, he reminds them—as God did in Malachi—that God is the Father to whom they should submit. More than that, Jesus claims to be his Son and to be speaking in one accord with the Father:

> "You know neither me nor my Father," Jesus answered. "If you knew me, you would also know my Father." He spoke these words by the treasury, while teaching in the temple.

But no one seized him, because his hour had not yet come. (John 8:19–20)

Jesus accuses them again later of not knowing God as Father: "'We have one Father—God.' Jesus said to them, 'If God were your Father, you would love me, because I came from God and I am here. For I didn't come on my own, but he sent me'" (8:41–42). Years upon years later, the Jewish people were still denying God as their Father, trading in obedience to his covenant for lesser things.

For anyone who reads Malachi, the obvious need is for a faithful priest and a faithful nation to rise up out of the ashes of Israel's blunders. And because Israel is made up of sinners doomed to fail, even with their best intentions, they are reminded that their covenant-keeping God would be the one to redeem them and keep his promises to them.

I mentioned above that God himself did just that—the eternal Son putting on flesh and dwelling (literally, "tabernacling") among us. The author of Hebrews tells us later in the canon that Jesus was the great high priest that Israel and indeed all the nations had been waiting for:

Now if perfection came through the Levitical priesthood (for on the basis of it the people received the law), what further need was there for another priest to appear, said to be according to the order of Melchizedek and not according to the order of Aaron? For when there is a change of the priesthood, there must be a change of law as well. For the one these things are spoken about belonged to a different tribe. No one from it has served at the altar. Now it is evident that our Lord came from Judah, and Moses said nothing about that tribe concerning priests.

And this becomes clearer if another priest like Melchizedek appears, who did not become a priest based on a legal regulation about physical descent but based on the power of an indestructible life. For it has been testified: "You are a priest forever according to the order of Melchizedek." So the previous command is annulled because it was weak and unprofitable (for the law perfected nothing), but a better hope is introduced, through which we draw near to God. (Heb 7:11–19)

The author of Hebrews points out here that something better had to come than merely another Levite priest. As I mentioned above, that covenant was broken and God was looking ahead at something new and better. Jesus is, thus, not another Levite priest trying to white-knuckle his way to obedience, but rather from a totally different line—the line of Melchizedek.

Not much is known about Melchizedek, given that he is briefly mentioned in Scripture in Genesis 14. We only know that he is a king-priest with a unique lineage, and he is drawn on by the author of Hebrews several times and Psalm 110 as a shadow of the coming Messiah. The author of Hebrews doesn't spend any time speculating about Melchizedek's origins—he simply uses his non-Levitical origin to show that Jesus is the king-priest who has brought a new priesthood and a new covenant. This was extremely good news to those who looked back at Malachi's day and looked around them in the present day, wondering what God was up to in the midst of the broken temple system. The covenant-keeping God of the OT had kept his promises in the person and work of the Son.

Gratefulness for the New Priesthood and Covenant

As post-NT Christians reading the entire biblical storyline, we are afforded the ability to look back at what Christ has done as the fulfillment and deliverer of the covenant promises of the covenant-keeping God. The temple is no longer a place where we are required to gather; instead, we are the temples of God by the indwelling of the Holy Spirit (1 Cor 3:16–17). Jesus himself replaced the temple, torn down and raised up as a fulfillment of the sacrificial system and ascended into heaven as our great interceding High Priest (John 2:21–22; Rom 8:34; Heb 9:12).

May we turn from idols and look to our God, who has kept his promises thus far and will keep his promise of final redemption (Revelation 21–22).

8

Eternal Manna and Water: John 7

I n this text, the sensibilities are worked out in similar ways to the passages we've covered thus far. First, we once again consider the letter and history. We pay attention to the context of the Gospel of John as a way to help offer guardrails to possible meanings. For example, John offers a purpose statement in John 20. How might that play into our interpretation?

By paying attention to the way the words go, we then consider what theological and Christological unity is present. In Numbers 16–17 and Malachi 1–2, we considered how the biblical story moves forward in history to how Christ might fulfill the story. In John 7, we ask the same question but in the other direction, considering what OT stories or motifs are present. In particular, we are given a cornucopia of references and allusions to OT texts that obviously inform the way Jesus speaks to the crowd.

Finally, when considering the personal and ecclesial application, we are driven by the text to properly respond to Jesus's command. His purpose statement in chapter 20 and the repeated interactions between Jesus and various interlocutors provides impetus for certain types of application. So we do not need to make up an application or dig around for nuggets of moral principles; instead, the text readily provides the context for us.

Introduction

At the end of his Gospel, John gives us a purpose statement for the book: "Jesus performed many other signs in the presence of his disciples that are not written in this book. But these are written so that you may believe that Jesus is the Messiah, the Son of God, and that by believing you may have life in his name" (John 20:30–31). So everything John does—God does—throughout his Gospel is for this purpose: that we may believe Jesus is the Messiah, the Son of God, and that by believing, we may have life in his name.

One of the primary ways John accomplishes this purpose is through portraits of Jesus's interactions with other people—Jewish leaders, the disciples, onlooking crowds, social outcasts, the sick and lame, etc. And these interactions help us understand what it means to believe in Jesus and have life in his name. In particular, we see that oftentimes, the Jewish leaders reject Jesus even though they are the ones who should first recognize him as the Messiah. How many times does he say something like, "Are you not a teacher of Israel's Scriptures?" (e.g., John 3) or "If you believed in Moses or Abraham, you would believe in me" (e.g., John 5)?

The Hebrew Scriptures pointed to and spoke of Jesus, creating a type of puzzle box cover that gives a portrait of who the Messiah was going to be. In turn, those who know the Hebrew Scriptures best should have been the ones who can mostly easily fit the pieces together, recognizing Jesus as the guy on the cover of the Messianic box. He is the one the OT has been pointing to (Luke 24:27, 44–47). And yet, with rare exceptions, the Jewish leaders do not believe.

On the other hand, it is the seemingly least expected people who believe in Jesus. The Samaritan woman, whom the Jews considered a half-breed subhuman who worships on the wrong mountain, told everyone she had met the Messiah (John 4:1–26). The lame man, who was ignored and cast out by his own people for thirty-eight years(!), proclaims Jesus's name (John 5:1–16).

In John 6, the disciples affirm Jesus as the word of life, that he is the manna from heaven come to provide for God's people. This sets the stage for John 7. We have a buffet of interactions and responses to Jesus:

- His brothers reject him in verses 1–9.
- The crowds are split about him in verses 10–36. Some say he's the Messiah, others that he has a demon (quite a juxtaposition).
- In the midst of it, the Jewish leaders are plotting against him.

Jesus uses these interactions to explain who he is. In particular, Jesus uses the occasion of a major Jewish festival to describe who he is. We will now focus on the crescendo of John 7 in verses 37–52:

On the last and most important day of the festival, Jesus stood up and cried out, "If anyone is thirsty, let him come to me and drink. The one who believes in me, as the Scripture has said, will have streams of living water flow from deep within him." He said this about the Spirit. Those who believed in Jesus were going to receive the Spirit, for the Spirit had not yet been given because Jesus had not yet been glorified.

When some from the crowd heard these words, they said, "This truly is the Prophet." Others said, "This is the Messiah." But some said, "Surely the Messiah doesn't come from Galilee, does he? Doesn't the Scripture say that the Messiah comes from David's offspring and from the town of Bethlehem, where David lived?" So the crowd was divided because of him. Some of them wanted to seize him, but no one laid hands on him.

Then the servants came to the chief priests and Pharisees, who asked them, "Why didn't you bring him?"

The servants answered, "No man ever spoke like this!"

Then the Pharisees responded to them, "Are you fooled too? Have any of the rulers or Pharisees believed in him? But this crowd, which doesn't know the law, is accursed."

Nicodemus—the one who came to him previously [John 3]—and who was one of them—said to them, "Our law doesn't judge a man before it hears from him and knows what he's doing, does it?"

"You aren't from Galilee too, are you?" they replied. "Investigate and you will see that no prophet arises from Galilee."

There's a lot to unpack here, but we can trace out three main questions that this text raises:

1. What is this "festival" mentioned here and why might it be important?
2. What is the Holy Spirit's relationship to Jesus and, by extension, those who believe in him?
3. What is the importance of "Galilee" in the Jews' rejection of Jesus?

What Is the Feast of Tabernacles?

The first question we might ask is, what is this "festival"? Back in John 7:2, we are told that they are celebrating the Feast of Tabernacles (or Tents / Booths / Shelters). We are told earlier in the chapter that this is why Jesus and his brothers and so many others had come to Judea—to celebrate this festival.

In short, the Feast of Tabernacles was a celebration of God's provision of the harvest, as well as a commemoration of God's provision for the Israelites in the wilderness. If we think back to John 6, Jesus compares himself to the manna that God sent from heaven while the Israelites were in the wilderness, so John has already primed us to think about the wilderness wanderings here.

John also says that this is the "last and most important day" of the festival. I do not think this detail is an accident, for two reasons. First, John tells us that he is selective in what he reports in his Gospel; second, if we go back to the OT to see what the Feast of Tabernacles is all about, we can look at Nehemiah 9 for some clarity on the context of this passage.

In Nehemiah 9, the Levites stand before the Israelites at the end of the festival and recount not only God's goodness, but also Israel's rejection of God's goodness. We can focus on the crescendo of the story in Neh 9:16–21 for our purposes here:

But our ancestors acted arrogantly;
they became stiff-necked and did not listen to your
commands.
They refused to listen
and did not remember your wonders
you performed among them.
They became stiff-necked and appointed a leader
to return to their slavery in Egypt.
But you are a forgiving God,
gracious and compassionate,
slow to anger and abounding in faithful love,
and you did not abandon them.
Even after they had cast an image of a calf
for themselves and said,
"This is your god who brought you out of Egypt,"
and they had committed terrible blasphemies,
you did not abandon them in the wilderness
because of your great compassion.
During the day the pillar of cloud
never turned away from them,
guiding them on their journey.
And during the night the pillar of fire
illuminated the way they should go.
You sent your good Spirit to instruct them.
You did not withhold your manna from their mouths,
and you gave them water for their thirst.
You provided for them in the wilderness forty years,
and they lacked nothing.

So, at the end of the festival in Nehemiah 9, the Israelites are reminded that God is good and faithful, and they are warned not to become stiff-necked and rebellious against God like their ancestors. God provided manna and water to them, and that should have been their clue to trust him, yet they rebelled.

In John 7, Jesus stands before the stiff-necked Jewish leaders and tells them that when they reject him, they are rejecting the God of Israel. Jesus is the manna (as he says in John 6), and the Spirit is the water (as he says here). God's provision—ultimately his salvation—stands before these Israelite leaders, commanding them to feast on the manna of Christ and drink the water of the Spirit.

God's provision of the manna and water in the wilderness—what was being commemorated annually in the Feast of the Tabernacles—was now standing in front of them. God the Son, the manna from heaven, was sent from the Father to tell them to believe in him and to receive God the Holy Spirit, the water—that they may have eternal life, eternal rest, eternal satisfaction. In John 4, Jesus tells the Samaritan woman that he offers eternal water that will make her never thirst again—that water is clarified in John 7 as the sending of the Spirit. What was once a temporary physical provision of bread and water in the wilderness is now an eternal spiritual provision of salvation in Christ and the Spirit.

Why Is the Holy Spirit Important?

The second question, then, is the Holy Spirit's inclusion in all of this. Throughout John's Gospel—and indeed the whole NT—the Holy Spirit's work is always inseparable from the work of the Father

and Son. The Father, Son, and Spirit's work in salvation is so inseparable, in fact, that Jesus will say in John 16 that it is "better for
him to go away" so that they can receive the Spirit. That feels like a
weird statement—it is better for Jesus to go away.

Jesus, God in the flesh, the obedient Second Adam, who died
for our sins, rose from the dead to give us new life, ascended to
heaven to be our mediator—he must go away? But that's the point:
his work cannot be separated from the Spirit's. Christ and the Spirit
nourish and water our wandering souls—they are God's provision
for us. The Father sends the Son and Spirit. So there is no salvation apart from Christ and the Spirit. Salvation has a Trinitarian
shape. Here is just a quick selection of how the Bible talks about
the Holy Spirit:

- In Genesis 1, the Spirit is God's presence hovering over
  the waters.
- In Joel 2, God's Spirit is promised to be poured out for
  salvation (fulfilled in Acts 2).
- Matthew 1 tells us that Mary conceived Jesus by the Spirit.
- Jesus says in John 3 that the Holy Spirit brings new birth
  and in John 14–16 that the Spirit will remind us of Jesus's
  words, be our Counselor or Advocate, etc.
- In Romans 8, Paul says the Spirit brings our adoption as
  children and even prays on our behalf.
- In 1 Corinthians 2, Paul says the Spirit gives us the wisdom
  to understand God.
- In 1 Corinthians 3, Paul says the Spirit makes us temples
  of God.

- In Ephesians 1, Paul says the Spirit is the deposit and seal of our salvation.
- In Galatians 5, Paul tells us the Spirit produces the fruit of salvation in us.
- In 2 Peter 1, Peter says the prophets spoke by the Spirit, all Scripture inspired by the Spirit.

In sum, then, we need Christ's work to absolve us of our sins and give us new life, so that we might receive his Spirit and become his children, his temples, to hear God's words and live according to his ways. They are told to come to Christ in order to receive the Spirit.

Whether we are talking about creation, revelation, salvation, sanctification, incarnation, and all the other theological -ations, the Spirit is always present and always working. The Holy Spirit—fully divine and acting in one accord with and inseparably from the Father and Son—is necessary for salvation.

As Neh 9:20 says, long before Pentecost, as the Israelites were wandering in the wilderness, "You sent your good Spirit to instruct them. You did not withhold your manna from their mouths, and you gave them water for their thirst." And Jesus tells the Israelites, "The manna and water—Son and Spirit—have come to offer you salvation. Don't turn away like your ancestors; feast and drink that you may have eternal life."

As the story progresses, the leaders do not respond the way they should; they do not heed the warning of the Levites in Nehemiah 9 and Jesus in John 7. They are as stiff-necked as their ancestors. It comes to a head starting in verse 40.

Why Reject Jesus Because of Galilee?

The third question we can ask is, what is the importance of Galilee as a reason for the Jews' rejection of Jesus? While it seems a little odd to point out his hometown, we see this question back in John 1:45–46:

> Philip found Nathanael and told him, "We have found the one Moses wrote about in the law (and so did the prophets): Jesus the son of Joseph, from Nazareth."
> "Can anything good come out of Nazareth [which is in Galilee]?" Nathanael asked him.
> "Come and see," Philip answered.

The truth is, there is no good biblical data that any of the OT prophets came from Galilee. Some think perhaps Jonah is from that region, but that is highly disputed. So can a prophet—or anything good—come from a rundown place like Galilee?

When I was in high school, I loved a country-rock band called Cross Canadian Ragweed, who had a popular song called "17," in which they complained, "You're always seventeen in your hometown." Jesus experiences something like this. In John 6 they say, "Isn't this Jesus, whose mother and father we know?" Here they say, "Can anything good come from Galilee?" and "We are the authorities, we know this guy and we reject him, that should be enough for you."

Notice that they also ask about the Messiah coming from David's line and being from Bethlehem. Matthew 1–2, for example, tell us that Jesus is from David's line and born in Bethlehem. That is not very disputed. But notice that the Jewish leaders really home in on that Galilee piece. Again, if we search the OT for important people coming out of Galilee, we do not find a long list. But one of the most important OT passages about the coming Messiah might help us here. Isaiah 9 contains a packed list of promises about the coming Messiah and God's work through him.

The character described in Isaiah 9 sounds just like Jesus:

- "The people walking in darkness have seen a great light; a light has dawned on those living in the land of darkness."
- "You will shatter their oppressive yoke."
- "A child will be born to us, a Son will be given."
- "The government will be upon his shoulders."
- "He will reign on David's throne; he will establish a kingdom of justice and righteousness."
- "He will be called Wonderful Counselor and Prince of Peace."

That's obviously prophesying about Jesus. In fact, in John 8:12 Jesus uses this light/dark language from Isaiah 9: "Jesus spoke to them again: 'I am the light of the world. Anyone who follows me will never walk in the darkness but will have the light of life.'"

Now here is the kicker: Isa 9:1 prefaces this Messianic figure and his work with this: "In the future God will bring honor to the way of the sea, to the land east of the Jordan, and to Galilee of the nations." So, perhaps no other prophet came from Galilee—but whoever this guy is in Isaiah 9, he will. He will bring honor to Galilee, the very place all of these people are dishonoring. In a broader sense, he will bring honor to all who are dishonored, justice to those who are oppressed, sight to all who are blind, life to all who are dead and buried in the darkness of their sins and trespasses. By trying to discredit Jesus through his Galilean heritage, the leaders actually reinforce who he is. He is David's heir from Bethlehem and the one who would bring honor to Galilee.

Believing in His Name

After asking if anything good can come from Nazareth/Galilee, Nathanael's story in John 1 ends this way:

> Then Jesus saw Nathanael coming toward him and said about him, "Here truly is an Israelite in whom there is no deceit."
>
> "How do you know me?" Nathanael asked.
>
> "Before Philip called you, when you were under the fig tree, I saw you," Jesus answered.
>
> "Rabbi," Nathanael replied, "You are the Son of God; you are the King of Israel!" (vv. 47–49)

There is no doubt that good biblical interpretation would have helped these leaders. But this story ultimately is not a question about biblical interpretation—whether or not the Jews remembered or rightly interpreted Nehemiah 9 or Isaiah 9—but rather a question of belief and unbelief. Their unbelief, their self-protection, clouded their vision.

Think about the juxtaposition: Nathanael wanted to know the answer to his question and Jesus said he had "no deceit in him." His question was pure. Nathanael modeled what the Christian tradition has called "faith seeking understanding."

The Jewish leaders, however, sought to protect their own interests and to discredit Jesus. They, by all accounts, knew the Scriptures well enough to know that Jesus was racking up Messianic puzzle pieces that were emerging as his face on the cover of the box. Their unbelief and their concern for power caused them to reject the one they were supposed to be looking for.

So perhaps we could ask ourselves the question, are we or do we want to be Nathanael or the Jewish leaders? We all like to think that we are Nathanael. If we could just see Jesus with our own eyes, or if we could be there when he walked out of the tomb, or if he called us audibly by name, we would never doubt again. But that's not the truth, is it? Scripture shows us people who experience this and reject him anyway.

Reading Scripture is good in its own right, whether it makes you "feel" a certain way sometimes or not. Theology is good in its own right, because it helps us know the God who has revealed himself. But in our zeal for the Word, we should be careful to avoid being like these Jewish leaders, who know the Scriptures and yet reject the one in whom their meaning is found.

John accomplishes his stated purpose, that we would know Jesus is the Messiah, the Son of God, and have life in his name, by showing us how not to respond to Jesus. God ultimately is warning us not to be like the Israelites who reject God's provision by turning up our noses at the manna and water of Christ and the Spirit. God is a gracious God who never abandons his people. He invites us to come. Let's believe in Christ, receive the Spirit, and have life in his name.

9

Incarnate for Image-Bearers: Hebrews 2

Hebrews 2 offers a clear opportunity to practice the sensibilities because this passage, and Hebrews as a whole, pressures the exegete to grapple with a heavy dose of biblical theology in a relatively short amount of text. First, we consider the letter and history by paying close attention to Hebrews 2 in light of the rest of the book of Hebrews, as well as the author's use of the Greek translation of Psalm 8, which is a different reading than the Hebrew.

The theological-Christological thread is evident as the author introduces the humanity of Christ in light of the Bible's story about humanity, as well as the divinity of Christ laid out clearly in Hebrews 1. We see what the early church referred to as the "hypostatic union"—that Christ is two natures (fully divine and fully human) in one person (the Word made flesh). One cannot remotely understand Hebrews 2 without a robust theological-Christological sensibility.

Finally, in his discussion of Christ's humanity, the author of Hebrews provides the occasion to reflect deeply on the implications of Christ's sinless humanity for us sinners. In particular, we are invited to praise God for his provision of salvation through the humanity of the Son. Further, we are encouraged to live in obedience to the Lord in light of his obedience.

Introduction

Hebrews 2 can be broken up into two sections: 2:1–4 and 2:5–18. We will briefly look at the exhortation of the first section, and then spend the rest of our time in the second section, which is only 14 verses but probably five sermons worth of content.

In Hebrews 1, the author has made the claim that God has spoken by his Son, and that this Son is the God-man (and not an angel). He then tells his audience in chapter 4,

> Therefore, since the promise to enter his rest remains, let us beware that none of you be found to have fallen short. For we also have received the good news just as they did. But the message they heard did not benefit them, since they were not united with those who heard it in faith. For we who have believed enter the rest, in keeping with what he has said,
> "So I swore in my anger,
> 'They will not enter my rest,'"
> even though his works have been finished since the foundation of the world. For somewhere he has spoken about

the seventh day in this way: "And on the seventh day God rested from all his works." (4:1–4)

There is an urgency to this opening statement in Hebrews 2: the Son has come, and so the time to repent is now. And if one has already repented, then they should persevere in faith and obedience to God. The Israelites did not enter the "rest" because of their disobedience and because of the providence of God; Christians are now warned not to repeat that mistake of "falling short."

These warnings are sprinkled throughout the book of Hebrews, seemingly elevating in urgency and severity for those who continually reject Christ or become complacent in following him. We might read this and say with Rom 7:24, "What a wretched man I am! Who will rescue me from this body of death?" The author of Hebrews has the answer.

Looking to Christ

Three big questions arise from the next section in verses 5–18:

1. What is a human?
2. What does it mean for Jesus to be human or, as John 1 puts it, for the Word to become flesh and dwell among us?
3. What does it mean for us for Jesus to be human?

These questions will help us untangle the issues in this text and come to a clearer understanding of what this passage is aiming toward.

1. What is a human?

The author of Hebrews quotes part of Psalm 8, which asks a very good question: "What is man that you remember him?" Many of us tend to equate humanity with sinfulness. We think that what it really means to be human is to be sinful, broken, fallen, misguided, and bent toward disobedience. We often use this as an excuse for our sin: "What did you expect? I'm a human! Of course I sin!"

There's one sense in which this is fair enough: all of humanity is born into sin because of our father Adam. It separates us from God and brings death and destruction. Paul says this explicitly in Rom 5:12: "Sin entered the world through one man [Adam], and death through sin, in this way death spread to all people, because all sinned." And due to our awareness of our own sinfulness, we tend to ask the question "what is man that you remember him?" in a much more accusatory way: "How could God remember or care about a human like me?" We tend to think that to be a human is to be a worthless, sinful worm. We don't get to speak or think well of ourselves or humanity as a whole because we're sinners.

But sinfulness is not the definition of what it means to be human and, indeed, to sin is to act contrary to human nature. When we sin, we don't act human—we act inhumane. The whole context of Psalm 8 helps us better understand where the author of Hebrews is going:

> LORD, our Lord,
> how magnificent is your name throughout the earth!
> You have covered the heavens with your majesty.
> From the mouths of infants and nursing babies,
> you have established a stronghold
> on account of your adversaries
> in order to silence the enemy and the avenger.
> When I observe your heavens,
> the work of your fingers,

the moon and the stars,
which you set in place,
what is a human being that you remember him,
a son of man that you look after him?
You made him little less than God
and crowned him with glory and honor.
You made him ruler over the works of your hands;
you put everything under his feet:
all the sheep and oxen,
as well as the animals in the wild,
the birds of the sky,
and the fish of the sea
that pass through the currents of the seas.
LORD, our Lord,
how magnificent is your name throughout the earth!

Psalm 8 refers back to the first chapters of Genesis—the language between Psalm 8 and Genesis 1–2 is paralleled very clearly when you compare them side-by-side, and Genesis 1–2 is where we first see humanity as seated at the top of the creational food chain. There, humans are made in God's image, and at least part of what it means to be made in God's image is: (1) to "be fruitful and multiply" or to give life and spread God's image across the globe, and (2) to "subdue the earth" or to exercise dominion over it. We see this played out, for example, when Adam names the animals and works the ground.

Adam and Eve are rulers of creation (as Psalm 8 puts it) as God's image-bearers. No other creature gets such honor. In fact, one of Satan's great lies to Eve is that God doesn't want her to be like him (Genesis 3). This is false because she and her husband were more like God than anything in existence. To sin is to become less like God, not more like him.

Psalm 8, then, points to a hope that humanity will be restored to its rightful place. To be human is to be the pinnacle of God's creation—those who bear his image in creating life, in subduing the earth, and in revealing his glory to the ends of the earth. But sin marred the image and set us at odds with God's will and purpose for us and, indeed, for all of creation. The biblical storyline is then one long story about humanity worshipping creation and misplacing worship in a whole host of ways because, as Romans 3 tells us, sin has disordered our desires and directed our gaze away from God's will and glory. But Hebrews 2 says here that the hope in Gen 3:15, in Psalm 8, across the whole Bible has come in the person of Jesus, the God-man.

So what does it mean to be human? To be the pinnacle of God's creation as image-bearers.

2. What does it mean for Jesus to become human?

Scripture is abundantly clear that the Son of God became a man (e.g., John 1:1–18; Phil 2:5–11). And he is truly human in every way: he has a human body and soul, a human mind and will that aligns with the divine will, the need for food and rest, and so on. These are human qualities—even Adam and Eve before they sinned had bodies and souls and minds and wills and needed to eat and sleep. They were not self-sufficient beings.

And Adam and Eve were humans before they sinned—they were what humanity is supposed to be. So to be truly human does not mean to be a sinner. To be truly human, the way we were created to be, is to be sinless, to be obedient to God, to glorify him and worship him rightly, to do his will and reflect him as his image-bearers.

So when Scripture says the Son put on flesh and dwelled among us, it doesn't mean he became a sinner. It means he became a human—a true human. And, we can't forget, he is God who has become man. He is truly human, but he's not merely human. He did not stop being God in the incarnation, and we have numerous examples throughout the Gospels that he does and says things only God can say and do.

Hebrews 1 has already clarified that this one person, Jesus Christ, is truly the God who created all things and sustains all things and truly the man who bled and died for us (Heb 1:1–4). Jesus is not sometimes God and other times man, nor does he stop being God so that he can be a man (as though God could stop being God). No, he is the God-man.

With this in mind, the author of Hebrews turns to the reason for not neglecting God's salvation in 2:5–9:

> He has not subjected to angels the world to come that we
> are talking about. But someone somewhere has testified:
>> "What is man that you remember him,
>> or the son of man that you care for him?
>> You made him lower than the angels
>> for a short time;
>> you crowned him with glory and honor
>> and subjected everything under his feet."
> For in subjecting everything to him, he left nothing that
> is not subject to him. As it is, we do not yet see everything
> subjected to him. But we do see Jesus—made lower than
> the angels for a short time so that by God's grace he might

taste death for everyone—crowned with glory and honor because he suffered death.

Hebrews 1 has already made clear that Jesus is not an angel, which is probably why he opts for the Greek translation of Psalm 8—"made lower than the angels for a short time"—instead of the Hebrew rendering, "You made him little less than God." However, the meaning is essentially the same: the Son became a man and stepped down into our mess in the incarnation. He did this so that humanity could be restored to our rightful place: at the pinnacle of creation as God's image-bearers who rule over creation as those who have "everything under our feet" as co-heirs with him.

Our passage here says both that angels don't get this privilege of ruling over creation (he has not subjected to angels the world to come) and later in the passage that the Son didn't become an angel. Further, Paul says in 1 Cor 6:3 that we will "judge the angels," so ultimately humans are made to be higher than them. So, though in our sin we are in a sense lower than those angels who have not fallen, the Son has come down to us to raise us back to our rightful place.

Though we may not be sure all that "judging the angels" might entail, the point is that we are higher than all creatures, even heavenly beings like the angels. We have the privilege of God himself coming to rescue us; we have the privilege of eternal life with our Maker; we are the only creatures with the ability to repent of sin and turn back to God. When we die, we have the privilege among all creatures on earth of immediately being in the presence of God as we await the resurrection of our bodies. The sending of the Son reminds us how deeply and uniquely we are loved by God. He did not come incarnate as an angel or a dog or anything else in creation. The Son of God became man.

Hebrews then tells us a little more about how Jesus restores us to our rightful place:

> For in bringing many sons and daughters to glory, it was entirely appropriate that God—for whom and through whom all things exist—should make the pioneer of their salvation perfect through sufferings. For the one who sanctifies and those who are sanctified all have one Father. That is why Jesus is not ashamed to call them brothers and sisters, saying:
>
> > "I will proclaim your name to my brothers and sisters;
> > I will sing hymns to you in the congregation."
> > Again, "I will trust in him." And again, "Here I am with the children God gave me." (2:10–13)

So God does not just snap his fingers from somewhere "out there" to save us. No, God the Son steps into our mess to live the perfect human life that Adam and no other human would or could. The way he does that is through living a real human life, fraught with suffering and weakness.

Jesus really and truly suffers like a human—he feels pain, he feels hunger and fatigue, he weeps at the death of his friend Lazarus, he is abandoned by his friends, he is slandered and mocked by his enemies, and he knows what it is like to stand toe-to-toe with Satan. He is "not ashamed to call us his brothers and sisters" because he has become one of us. We are not too far gone to be the children of God. We are not worthless worms with no hope. We have a big brother in Jesus who really and truly and meaningfully identifies with the frailties of human existence. And in our union with Christ, his perfect obedience and sacrifice in our place brings us up with him to the honor and pride of place as God's image-bearers.

This passage is similar to Rom 8:14–17:

> For all those led by God's Spirit are God's sons. For you did not receive a spirit of slavery to fall back into fear. Instead, you received the Spirit of adoption, by whom we cry out, "Abba, Father!" The Spirit himself testifies together with our spirit that we are God's children, and if children, also heirs—heirs of God and coheirs with Christ—if indeed we suffer with him so that we may also be glorified with him.

Again, one can debate what it may mean to be "co-heirs" or to "judge angels," but it means at the very least that we as humans have a dignity and worth that surpasses anything else in creation. The incarnation is proof. The Image of God himself became an image-bearer to restore the image in us.

The author of Hebrews continues this for the rest of the chapter:

> Now since the children have flesh and blood in common, Jesus also shared in these, so that through his death he might destroy the one holding the power of death—that is, the devil—and free those who were held in slavery all their lives by the fear of death. For it is clear that he does not reach out to help angels, but to help Abraham's offspring. Therefore, he had to be like his brothers and sisters in every way, so that he could become a merciful and faithful high priest in matters pertaining to God, to make atonement for the sins of the people. For since he himself

has suffered when he was tempted, he is able to help those who are tempted. (2:14–18)

This phrase "he had to be like his brothers and sisters in every way" can be a little confusing. We might take this to mean that he is just like every human in every way. But this phrase is qualified and defined by the context of this passage and the broader biblical context. According to this passage, how is he "like us in every way"?

1.   He has flesh and blood.
2.   He experiences human suffering and ultimately death.

In short, then, "he himself suffered when he was tempted" does not mean that Jesus's "temptation" relates to struggling with sinning like fallen humans. There are at least five reasons why it is contrary to biblical teaching to say that Jesus's "temptations" mean that he desired to sin or wrestled with whether or not he should sin.

First, the word translated "temptation" (πειρασθείς) is sometimes translated as "testing." In the context of this passage, the "testing" Jesus experiences is related to his suffering as a human, not related to whether he may have sinned. We might think of this "testing" as him demonstrating that he is who he says he is; it is not a test that we hope he gets right but rather a test that proves to us that we need not doubt his perfection.

Second, this passage in its immediate context ties it to his suffering and atonement, not to what is going on in his mental faculties or his psyche. And even if we are to take the translation as "temptation," which is entirely justifiable, we know that we have to define words based on their context, both within the passage itself and within the rest of the biblical storyline.

Third, Jesus is never shown in Scripture to struggle with whether or not to sin. When he is tempted in Matthew 4 by Satan, you get no hint that he is wrestling with how to respond. Rather, he quotes Scripture, refutes Satan's every move, and tells him to go away. Hebrews says here he defeated Satan. Yes, Jesus feels hunger and fatigue; yes, he experiences grief and joy; yes, in the Garden of Gethsemane he feels the weight of preparing to bear God's wrath on the cross; yes, Satan brings external temptations to him. So he experiences temptation, but not like us. He does not waver on whether or not to sin. The Bible never indicates that Jesus has any other desire or purpose than to do the Father's will and steadfastly go to the cross. Hebrews 12:2 says, "For the joy that lay before him he endured the cross." In John 10, he says "nobody takes [my life] from me, but I lay it down on my own" (v. 18). He knew his purpose and had joy in it—even through his sufferings. There was no wavering.

Fourth, the promises of God will always come to pass. And perhaps the biggest promise from Gen 3:15 onward is that God would send a Deliverer. God, who keeps his promises and knows the beginning from the end, who created time and space itself, already knows the future. We never get any sense that we are going to be crossing our fingers about whether or not the coming Messiah would save us. The Scriptures must be fulfilled, Jesus says in Matthew 26 (in the same context as his asking for "this cup" to pass from him). So, for the Father to send his Son to play a game of chicken with Satan, hoping Jesus can hold off his temptations to sin long enough to save us, does not fit at all with the biblical storyline.

Fifth, Jesus is still God in the incarnation, which means he is morally perfect and unable to sin. The Bible says there are things that God cannot do. For example, the Bible says that God cannot be tempted to sin (Jas 1:13) and cannot lie (Titus 1:2). Jesus is both God and a truly obedient human born of a virgin, which means he does not have misguided and fallen desires like other humans. His humanity does not weaken his divinity; rather, it might be better to say that his divinity sanctifies or "strengthens" his humanity. He is still that same divine person in the incarnation (John 1:1–18; Phil 2:5–11). The eternal Son took on flesh and dwelt among us so that he could undo everything Adam (and we) has done. To say that for Jesus's "temptations" to be "real" he had to want to sin is to import our own ideas onto the biblical text. Jesus endured all frailty of humanity, died for our sins, bore the wrath of God, did it all with joy and without sin. This means that we should be trying to suffer faithfully like him, not thinking he has to suffer like us. He suffered to the point of death and never broke.

If we can get our minds and hearts around the idea that Jesus is truly human with desires always pointed in the right direction, not a fallen human with confused and twisted desires, we can better understand how and why he can save us and fulfill the promises of God in salvation.

3. What does it mean for us that Jesus is human?

Two helpful phrases from church history can help make this plain. Irenaeus of Lyons said, "The Son of God became a Son of Man so that . . . we could become sons of God."[1] In other words, the goal of the incarnation was not for the sinless Son to become like us fallen sinners, but for we fallen sinners to become like the sinless

---

[1] *AH* 3.19. My rendering.

Son. Gregory of Nazianzus offers a similar axiom: "What is not assumed is not healed."[2] In other words, he became truly human in every way to heal humanity in every way—body, soul, and so forth. He was not kind of human or partly human; no, he became truly human to make us truly human.

Sometimes we wonder if God really loves us, if he really forgives us, or if he is really there when we are suffering. The author of Hebrews says to look to Jesus and cling to his salvation. We as human beings are the pinnacle of God's creation. The Father loves us so much that "He gave His only begotten Son, that whoever believes in Him should not perish but have everlasting life" (John 3:16 NKJV). All the work was done in the Son's sinless life, atoning and substitutionary death, glorious resurrection, and ascension to the right hand of the Father. And right now that same Jesus stands in heaven as the high priest who, Hebrews 7 says, lives to intercede for us.

The author says in Heb 2:8 that "we do not yet see everything subjected to him"—there's still sin and death and brokenness all around us—but we do see Jesus, the faithful high priest who has conquered sin and death so that we can have a hope and a future in eternity with him, when there is no more sin, no more tears, no more brokenness, as Revelation 21 promises.

We do not need a Savior who is just a little less broken than us. We do not need a good moralist who was able to white-knuckle good works for thirty years and thankfully not sin before he got to the cross. If so, that would indicate that all the promises of God were hanging in the balance and God was hoping Jesus would make it to the finish line.

---

[2] *Ep.* 101. My rendering.

We need the Savior who was promised by God and longed for by Moses and the prophets and the psalmists, the Savior who is the God-man who is both able to forgive our sins and able to suffer human existence all the way to death to be our substitute. Jesus is the Plan A of salvation. His ministry was assured, his eyes always on the cross, his steadfast willingness to save us never in question. And whether he is preparing his disciples for his departure or arguing with the Jewish leaders about his identity, he reminds them that the incarnation was promised beforehand and sure to accomplish its goal. Hebrews 4 says that Jesus "has been tempted in every way as we are, yet without sin," and that "yet without sin" half-sentence means everything when it comes to our salvation.

To be truly human is to be like Jesus, not like us right now. The good news is that God became man to do everything we could not. He is the pioneer of our faith. The true faithful human. May we cling to that salvation.

CONCLUSION:
ANCIENT HERMENEUTICS
FOR THE MODERN CHURCH

This book has argued that modern Christians need to retrieve premodern interpretation by remembering the three sensibilities Christians have generally shared across the Christian tradition. First, we need to remember the way the scriptural words go. Our interpretation is biblical insofar as we care about the claims of the text as God's self-revelation to us. Second, we need to remember that Scripture has a theological-Christological unity. This unity is predicated upon the claims of Scripture itself: it is one divine revelation and is self-referential through quotes, allusions, fulfillment of promises, and so forth. Our interpretation is biblical insofar as it takes seriously the divine author's providential ordering of Scripture and its intricately intertwined claims from Genesis to Revelation. Third, we need to remember that Scripture is oriented to personal and communal transformation as the Holy Spirit illuminates our hearts and minds to transform us into the image of Christ. I demonstrated these three sensibilities through examples from church history across the patristic, medieval, and Reformation eras of the Christian tradition. It was important to note that there are obvious and important distinctions not only between eras of church history, but even between figures within these eras. Nonetheless, close readings of Scripture have pressured Christians in all times and places to ask questions related to these three sensibilities. Indeed, it is easy to show throughout church history that these three sensibilities inform a basic Christian reading of Scripture.

I recognize that the second part of the book, "Practicing the Sensibilities," can be a bit idiosyncratic since the examples in each chapter represent the way I personally would work out teaching or preaching these texts. I don't expect readers of this book to find these expositions particularly unique or insightful; rather, I hope they model one example of how the premodern sensibilities address the major questions one should ask when reading Scripture. Ultimately, I hope they encourage you to practice the sensibilities for yourself.

God providentially gives us a great cloud of historical witnesses. By looking back on our heritage as an exercise in humility, accountability, and encouragement, I pray that modern Christians will see these witnesses as indispensable aids in reading and applying Scripture's truths in our own time. May we all say with Augustine, "*Tolle lege!*"—"Take up and read!"[1]

---

[1] *Conf.* 8.12.29.

NAME INDEX

A

Allen, Michael, 30
Austen, Jane, 7
Ayres, Lewis, 16, 36, 71

B

Barkley, Gary Wayne, 38
Behr, John, 40, 45, 68, 91, 115
Beinert, W. A., 38
Bingham, D. Jeffrey, 71
Blowers, Paul M., 18
Boyle, John F., 25
Bright, Pamela, 21

C

Cameron, Michael, 20–21
Cavadini, John C., 18
Chadwick, Henry, 95
Chase, Frederic H., Jr., 99

D

Dauphinais, Michael, 25, 77–78
De Lubac, Henri, 17, 22, 38–39
Dockery, David S., 3
Donaldson, James, 69
Duesing, Jason G., 24

E

Emerson, Matthew Y., 117
Ernest, James D., 72, 76

F

Fairbairn, Donald, 45–46
Falls, Thomas B., 90
Fink, David C., 30
Finn, Nathan A., 24
Ford, David F., 74

G

Gamble, Richard C., 80
George, Timothy, 3, 112
Gilhooly, John R., ix, 78
Gurry, Peter J., 17

H

Hagen, Kenneth, 58
Hains, Todd R., 30
Halton, Thomas P., 47, 49
Harkins, Franklin T., 24
Haroutunian, Joseph, 81
Heine, Ronald E., 42
Helmer, Christine, 62
Hill, Robert C., 47, 49

SUBJECT INDEX

A

Abraham (biblical figure), 20, 41, 49–51, 152, 174
Adam and Eve (biblical figures), 59, 169–70
Alexandrian reading culture, 17–19
allegory, 4–5, 10, 17–26, 29–30, 37, 42–46, 48, 50–51, 53–57, 63–64, 67, 76–77, 80, 82–83, 109, 111
  Antiochene view of, 46
  Augustine's view of, 19–21
  as dangerous method, 82, 110
  John Calvin's view of, 82
  John Chrysostom's view of, 46–48
  Luther's view of, 26, 29–30
  Nicholas of Lyra's view of, 26
  Origen's view of, 37–38, 42–45
  Theodore of Mopsuestia's view of, 45
  Victorine school's view of, 24
Andrew of Caesarea, 66
Andrew of Saint Victor, 24. *See also* Victorine School, the
angels, 56, 103, 166, 171–72, 174
Anglicanism, 6
Antiochene reading culture, 17–19, 45–47. See also *historia*; John

Chrysostom; Theodore of Mopsuestia; *theoria*
Apelles (student of Marcion), 43. *See also* Gnosticism; Marcion
apologetics, 35, 91
Aquinas, Thomas, 21, 24–25, 34, 67, 71, 77–79, 84
  on Psalm 8, 78–79
  on the unity of Scripture, 77–79
  and the senses of Scripture, 77
archaeology, 34
Arius, 19
Arminius, Jacobus, 5
artificial intelligence, 116
Athanasius of Alexandria, 67, 72–77, 84, 100, 115
  Against the Arians, 72–76
  extant works of, 72
  On the Incarnation, 115
  and Proverbs 8, 73–76
  and the "scope" of Scripture, 72–77
atonement, 130–31, 135, 174–75
Augustine of Hippo, 19–21, 24–25, 30, 80–81, 90, 94–99, 107, 111, 182
  and the dual loves, 95
  Confessions, 95–97
  Retractions, 95

Gregory of Nazianzus, 73, 178
Gregory the Great, 21

H

Hadrian of Canterbury, 23
Hagar (biblical figure), 48–53
heresy, 99, 114
Hexapla, 35. *See also* Origen of
Alexandria
historia (interpretive principle),
46–47, 50
historical theology, 113–14
Holy Spirit, the
divinity of, 3, 19
as illuminator, 2, 40–41, 46,
80, 84
and inseparable operations,
157–59
as teacher, 1–2
Hosea (prophet), 145
Hugh of Saint Victor, 23–24, 37,
53–57, 63–64. *See also* Victorine
School
Didascalicon, 54, 56
on Genesis, 56–57
On Sacred Scripture, 53
on the Pentateuch, 54–56
on the Trinity, 56–57
humility, 114–15, 182
hypostatic union, 165–66

I

icons, 99
idolatry, 78, 89, 93, 134, 145, 149
image of God, 56–57, 100, 102,
116, 169–72, 174
imitation, 55, 136
imputed righteousness, 62
interpretation of the Bible, modern,
4–5, 34–36, 66–67
interpretation of the Bible, premodern, 2–8

as dangerous, 109–10
eschatological impulse of, 89–90
habitus of, 6–7
in the Medieval era, 22–27
in the Patristic era, 14–21
in the Reformation era, 27–31
understanding of "history", 35
Irenaeus of Lyon, 15–16, 35, 43,
67–71, 76, 84, 177–78. *See
also* canon, biblical: unity of
the; Gnosticism; rule of faith;
Valentinianism
Against Heresies, 69–70
On the Apostolic Preaching,
68–69
Isaac (biblical figure), 49, 52
Isidore of Seville, 24
Islam, 99

J

Jerome, 24, 30, 35
Jesus Christ
divinity of, 3, 19
as fulfillment of philosophy,
91–94
as high priest, 135–36
humanity, 170–79
incarnation of, 20
resurrection of. *See* resurrection:
of Jesus Christ
as Second Adam, 158
as teacher, 1–2
John Cassian, 21, 26
John Chrysostom, 17–19, 23, 37,
45–53, 63, 66, 80, 83, 100. *See
also* allegory: John Chrysostom's
view of
on circumcision, 50, 52
on God's power, 50
on God's providence, 49–50
homilies on Galatians, 48–53
homilies on Genesis, 47–53

SCRIPTURE INDEX